AUTHOR	CLASS
BERTRAM, J.	739.52 ✗
TITLE	No.
Lost brasses.	420188088

LOST BRASSES

FRONTISPIECE

John and Joan Havelde, 1498, St Mary Magdalen's, Oxford - a drawing by
Hinton of a fine composition of the Trinity with saints. Reproduced by
courtesy of the Bodleian Library

LOST BRASSES

JEROME BERTRAM

DAVID & CHARLES

NEWTON ABBOT LONDON
NORTH POMFRET (VT) VANCOUVER

By the same author
BRASSES AND BRASS RUBBING IN ENGLAND

IN MEMORIAM

CHARLES STONOR
Exegi monumentum aere perennius . . .

420188088
ISBN 0 7153 7141 X
Library of Congress Catalog Card Number 75-43208

© Jerome Bertram 1976

Set in 11 on 13pt Times
and printed in Great Britain
by Redwood Burn Limited
Trowbridge and Esher
for David & Charles (Publishers) Limited
Brunel House   Newton Abbot   Devon

Published in the United States of America
by David & Charles Inc
North Pomfret   Vermont 05053   USA

Published in Canada
by Douglas David & Charles Limited
1875 Welch Street   North Vancouver   BC

CONTENTS

PREFACE

One may well ask what is the point of studying lost brasses, as if there were not enough surviving ones to get on with. Most people find it surprising that we can find out anything about lost brasses, and once reassured that we can, imagine it to be an erudite and boring study. In fact, not only is the actual detective work of discovering lost brasses fascinating in its own right but the knowledge we gain from them can make a significant difference to our appreciation of brasses in general.

An indent or matrix that has lost its brass may look dull and unimportant, but once we set to work we can deduce an astonishing amount from the bare outlines in the stone, and after what can be an enthralling trail of discovery through old books and papers, we can often clothe the bare stone with a named and dated brass, reconstructed in every detail. Once we know just how much these stones can tell us, there is a new interest in looking round old churches.

This book is designed to unveil the mysteries of the brasses we have lost-to explain how they came to be lost, how they can be reconstructed from indents and documents, and how important a contribution this knowledge can make to the now very popular study of brasses in general. If this study of brasses is to be taken seriously by archaeologists or art historians, it must include the evidence on those now lost, which so drastically alters the pattern of distribution of brasses and can corroborate or correct our generalisations.

There are still a great many indents unrecorded, a great many documents unsearched, but, as this book attempts to show, the work is not difficult or tedious if enough people can be inspired to undertake it for their own parish or district.

J.F.A.B.
Oxford 1975

1

INTRODUCTION

And some there be, which have no memorial . . .
(*Ecclesiasticus,* 44,9)

Brasses have been studied in a scholarly and archaeological way for many years, and no serious writer on the subject has failed to comment on the number that once existed and are now lost, or on the importance of empty indents-the matrices or casements left after brasses have been removed. Time and again writers have finished their account of 'Protestant pilfery or Puritan pillage' with a recommendation that more care be taken of surviving indents, and that they be properly recorded. Nevertheless, by and large, this recommendation has been ignored. Individual indents have been illustrated, and occasionally records or at least lists of the indents of a particular county or area have been made, but no consistent work has been done on lost brasses, and very little effort has ever been concentrated on bringing together the archaeological evidence of indents and the documentary evidence of old books and manuscripts.

The Rev H. W. Macklin, addressing the Oxford Society in 1899, said, 'The value of despoiled slabs was hardly recognised by the brass-rubbers who first raised the study of monumental brasses to the rank of a distinct branch of archaeology . . . of mere matrices they had no time to take account.'[1] The point is largely valid even today.

7

If the study of brasses is to be treated seriously as a branch of archaeology-the discipline of chalcology rather than mere brass-rubbing-we must include the lost examples. No modern archaeologist when writing a report would ignore the post holes or robber trenches from which features have been removed, or any documentary evidence that could throw light on them. In the same way the study of brasses can be greatly extended by recording and analysing indents, and collating them with other sources to obtain as complete a record as possible of what has been lost.

Some people estimate that as much as 90 per cent of our brasses have been lost, but in fact only about 40 per cent of known brasses are lost, and those lost without trace would probably increase the percentage to 50. Nevertheless, as will be seen, many important categories of brass are either totally lost or very greatly diminished.

If we are to study brasses with the idea of producing general conclusions, it is obvious that the larger the sample the better, and it would be unscientific to ignore over a third of the available evidence, that of indents and documents, especially if it can be shown that it would make a significant difference to the whole. Surviving brasses have been well listed-extremely thoroughly for the period before 1700-though new discoveries are still being made. Later brasses and also indents are now being listed by the Monumental Brass Society, and this work will take many years. However, mere lists are not enough: to do any serious work it is necessary to have some sort of reproduction of each indent. For surviving brasses such reproductions are available in the great brass-rubbing collections of Cambridge and London, but there is not yet anything like an adequate collection of rubbings or drawings of indents. Those that have been published have to be ferreted out of a wide variety of books and journals, though in fact simply collating published sources provides a reasonable picture of what has been lost, and the evidence can then be compared with that from surviving brasses.

If all the indents in Britain were recorded, and all the possible documentary sources thoroughly searched, the list of lost brasses would rival that of the survivors. It is the author's hope that this will eventually be achieved. Only then shall we be sure that chalcologists are working from something like all the examples, rather than from an unrepresentative sample. It is the aim of this book to show how such a list can be compiled, and to illustrate, in what must be only provisional conclusions, what differences the additional information will make to the general study of brasses.

On the whole the scope of this book has had to be confined to brasses in the British Isles (in their traditional counties), simply because so little work has ever been done on Continental lost brasses. We know from indents, and the drawings made for Roger de Gaignières, that a large number of very fine brasses once existed in France, but hardly a dozen of any importance survive now. To search the whole of Europe for indents would be a superhuman task; documentary sources could be found in many countries, and more languages, but the destruction of records as well as of original brasses has been much greater than in Britain. The author has noticed indents in churches from Novgorod to Budapest, and the number found on chance visits shows that a systematic search of all churches would be very rewarding. There is a fine Tournai marble indent in the Mariacki at Gdańsk, a well-preserved indent for a crozier brass in the church of the Knights of Malta at Prague, an early Lombardic inscription indent built into the walls of Bratislava cathedral, many more in Austria and the Tyrol, several in Laon cathedral, and even an indent to an early governor at Jamestown, Virginia.[2] There may well be indents (or even surviving brasses) in the eastern Mediterranean dating from the last of the Crusader kingdoms. All these must remain for later systematic recording, as must the searching of documents in everything from Latin to mediaeval Hungarian.

The idea for this book largely grew out of work in which the author was involved with the Oxford University Archaeological Society during 1972-3. It began as a simple count of indents for the Monumental Brass Society's listing programme, but developed into the first systematic catalogue of lost brasses from a whole city. Drawing techniques were evolved and documentary sources collated. Eventually the whole was published, with illustrations of all the indents except those showing inscriptions only or those too fragmentary to be of any value.[3] Doubtless improvements and modifications to the method and format should be made, but in general it is hoped that the Oxford survey will serve as a model for others, eventually to cover the whole country.

It is one of the ironies of history that a flimsy piece of paper is more durable than brass or stone. This book is to a great extent a witness to this: many indents mentioned here will doubtless disappear in the future, and this will be their only record. Records of some brasses of which no indents survive have been preserved by the most tenuous links-a scribble on the back of an envelope, a note on the flyleaf of a prayer book. The most casual notes are of value, and one should never lose an opportunity of recording or sketching indents, however hurriedly, lest they be lost before anyone has time to record them properly.

Notes for this chapter appear on page 185

2

HOW BRASSES WERE LOST

Some of these brasses have disappeared. Of others portions
have been lost. Others have been removed from their slabs, or
their slabs have been removed to parts of the church where
they were not before, in order that the *hic jacet* might lie like
an epitaph (Ralph Griffin)

People often assume that brasses now lost were simply worn
away by brass-rubbers, or were pulled up by Cromwell; but
even the most ardent churchman has to admit that the sixteenth-century Reformation was mostly responsible. It is
interesting that Newman in his introduction to Dowsing's
journal cites it as evidence that church desecration was not
confined to the sixteenth century but also took place during
the Civil War, countering the opposite error, which is more
prevalent today. The normal account of how brasses have
been lost (including, it must be admitted, the author's own
views in *Brasses and Brass Rubbing in England*) must be corrected in many ways. We are often told that such and such a
brass was destroyed during the Civil War, despite evidence to
prove it was lost a century earlier or later. Of course brasses
were destroyed during the war and the Commonwealth, but
they have been destroyed at every period of English history.
Naturally the later the destruction the more complete the evidence, for the distribution of evidence is very much the same
as the distribution of recorders. Few brasses can have been

lost this century of which rubbings do not survive, whereas in the earlier period we must rely largely on chance references.

Very few brasses were destroyed by genuine accident. The vast majority were victims of human neglect or greed, prompted or encouraged by different historical circumstances.

THE MIDDLE AGES

It is normally assumed that brasses were respected throughout the Middle Ages, and that all the brasses ever laid remained in perfect condition until the Reformation. While it is true that we have very little evidence for mediaeval destruction of brasses, they must have been lost and mutilated quite as frequently then as later. Obviously accidental wear and damage were inevitable, and most of the thirteenth- and early fourteenth-century brasses were probably already badly mutilated by the close of the Middle Ages. Delicate cross stems and openwork tracery in canopies, separate-letter inscriptions, small shields and devices held in place by no more than a layer of pitch, were liable to work loose under the ordinary pressure of feet, and once loose would have been swept up and thrown away. Even riveted plates work loose under pressure, and few people during the Middle Ages would have taken any interest in them. One of the few records of the mediaeval attitude to brasses shows that the parish merely wanted to clear them out of the way: in 1511 the churchwardens of Minster in Sheppey, Kent, petitioned the Archbishop of Canterbury that 'it is desyred that where, of long tyme agoo, in the said chapell, a knight and his wife buried, and their pictures upon theym very sore worne and broken, that they may take away the pictures, and lay in the place a playn stone, with an epitaphy who is there buried, that the people may make setts and pewys, where they may more quietly serve God, and that it may less cowmber the roome.'[1] Luckily the Archbishop, Thomas Warham, was an educated man and refused their petition, since the brasses survive and were evidently repaired about that time. However, this act of respect to the dead was done at the expense of someone else, for the back of another brass was used to repair the male figure.

Even in the Middle Ages churches and chapels were from time to time made redundant, or destroyed by fire and never rebuilt. Oslo Museum has a few fragments of a very large Flemish brass that was virtually destroyed by fire in 1523,[2] and doubtless fire damage was common earlier. Brasses have been known to survive fires, but in most cases the loose plates would simply have been thrown away with the rubble.

Old tombs and slabs were sometimes appropriated as building material during the frequent rebuilding and extension of churches that went on throughout the period. Recently, during excavations at St. Paul's Cathedral, the foundations of the fifteenth-century cloister were found to incorporate a broken indent of a cross brass of about 1400. The indent had been used, as there were rivets in it, but it must have had a life of only 20 years or so before the brass was destroyed and it was reused.[3] On a larger scale, about 120 incised cross-slabs were found built into a wall of c1260 at Bakewell in Derbyshire. Old incised slabs are frequently found so built into walls, or used as pier bases, as at Cirencester.

Where churches and chapels were abandoned, the brasses seem to have been simply left for anyone to steal, as at Poynings, Sussex, where the south transept with five brasses was closed off and deserted about 1525. It is rare, however, to find brasses or indents in excavated churches that were abandoned in the Middle Ages, since, in villages so poor that even the church was deserted, it is unlikely that there was any family that could afford brasses.

Towards the end of the period we know of churches demolished to make way for ambitious building schemes, as at Cuddington in Surrey, which was cleared to provide a site for Nonsuch Palace in 1538. When the palace banqueting house was excavated in 1960, a number of indents were found built into the drainage system.[4] Many small religious houses were suppressed during the Middle Ages, and these must often have contained brasses. A brass from Holy Trinity Priory, London (suppressed in 1531), was sold off by Lord Audley and re-used to make a brass for Walter Curson and wife at the Austin Friary, Oxford. When the Friary in turn was suppressed, the brass was moved to its present home at Waterperry.[5]

Other cases of appropriated brasses are not uncommon during the Middle Ages. An example from one of Wolsey's suppressions is the brass of Thomas Wydville and his two wives, 1435, from St James's Convent, Northampton, which was re-used at Bromham, Bedfordshire, for Sir John Dyve, his wife and mother, in 1535. Other re-used brasses, which may have come from redundant churches or simply have been lifted from a church in use, were either turned over and re-engraved, like part of a military brass of c1330 on the back of a brass of 1435 at Cople, Bedfordshire, or simply given a new inscription, as at Ticehurst, Sussex, or Stockbury, Kent, where fourteenth-century figures were re-used in the early sixteenth-century. At Ticehurst, in fact, the widow Agnes Wybarne left money in her will of 1503 to 'bye a convenient stone' for the brass of her husband, herself and his first wife. Evidently the executors found the earlier brass and slab very convenient.[6]

Besides accidental and individual losses, in the Middle Ages, as ever since, the church authorities themselves did not scruple to convert their monuments into ready cash if possible. Langland complains of the friars who periodically cleared away all the floor slabs from their churches so that they could start again, charging a fee for each burial:

And in beldyng of toumbes   They traveileth grete
To chargen ther cherche flore   And chaungen it ofte.[7]

The sale of one brass was actually recorded on a new monument: Gough quotes an inscription in Vauluisanc Abbey, France, in memory of Anselm de Bercenay, Bishop of Laudun, 1238, which states that he originally had a copper

tomb but Abbot Henry sold it in 1448 to pay for church repairs, and replaced it with a stone monument.[8]

THE REFORMATION

Probably the heyday for the destruction of brasses was the
period covering the dissolution of the monasteries and the
gradual advance of Protestantism under Edward VI. The
number of brasses destroyed at this time is unknown, but
must have been phenomenal. Unfortunately we have few descriptions of the lost brasses, since no one troubled to record
inscriptions or describe monuments in the old monastic
churches. Leland gives a few hints, but the rest we must deduce from indents and brief notices in accounts of sales.

The biggest blow was of course the actual dissolution of the
monasteries. There were brasses in monastic churches commemorating not only monks, nuns and friars themselves but,
more frequently and more splendidly, benefactors of the
houses, nobles or merchants, even secular priests and
bishops, not to mention the host of monastic retainers and
their families, all of whom chose to be buried in a monastic
church rather than in their own parishes. The only monastic
church that retains any number of brasses is St Alban's, in
which nineteen brasses or fragments survive, and we know
from indents of at least another forty-eight now lost. Of these
only twenty-one were definitely monastic. St Alban's was one
of the richest abbeys in England, and was exceptional, but
even the smallest religious houses probably had several
brasses each, and some may have had more than now survive
in any English church.

When monastic churches remained standing, as did St
Alban's, most brasses were probably left alone for a time, as
the building would have continued to function with little
change. The majority of churches, however, were demolished
or converted into private houses, and from these the brasses
were almost invariably sold by the king's commissioners. It

was normal for the brasses, bells and lead to be sold before a monastery was handed over to its new owner, and there are records of this. For instance, at Darley in Staffordshire the metal from tombs and gravestones, with that from the roof of the church, aisles, etc, was sold for £20.[9] Sometimes brasses were moved into neighbouring churches, usually by relations of the people commemorated, as in the case of the Curson brass already mentioned, but occasionally by public bodies: for instance, the brass and coffin of Geoffrey Barbur, a benefactor to the town, were solemnly translated from Abingdon Abbey to the parish church of St Helen, by the mayor and council.

More frequently the brasses were bought up by workshops, re-engraved and laid as new brasses in a remarkably short time. The brass of Sir Anthony Fitzherbert, at Norbury, Derbyshire, was engraved in 1538 on the back of a rather fine brass to Thomas, Prior of Croxden, a house dissolved in the same year. Likewise part of a brass to Sir John Popham from the London Charterhouse was relaid at Reading in the year of dissolution. There seem to have been no scruples: in at least one case, at St Stephen's, Norwich, we find one of the dispossessed religious themselves commemorated on a piece of re-used monastic plunder.

Urban monastic sites were nearly always completely cleared and built over within a few years. The stone was sold off for building, and the paving slabs, including indents, were usually the first to go, as smooth flagstones could be more easily re-used than wall rubble or broken stone. For instance, at the Chelmsford Blackfriars the inventory includes, 'The pathement with gravestons in the quere chapellis and cherche with yᵉ eyarne and glase in those placeis xxxˢ'.[10] Excavated urban monastic churches are nearly always found to have been stripped of all their floor slabs even where tiling and wall footings remain, and with these slabs vanished the last evidence for many brasses. It is rare for an excavation to find brasses or slabs, except for the occasional loose Lombardic

16

letter-too small to have been worth taking up when the brasses were reaved-which may simply have fallen out of the slabs as they were being jacked up and carted out. Eight such letters, which must have come from at least three different brasses, were found in the Oxford Blackfriars.

In the country, monasteries were often merely abandoned once the metal had been salvaged, and indents have quite often been found in remote ruins such as Fountains, Byland or Salley Abbeys.

Indents and incised slabs removed from monastic churches have been put to odd uses: one, a cross slab from Abingdon, was found about 1810 set on edge and serving as a stile on a footpath between Abingdon and Radley;[11] another, an incised slab from Netley, formed part of the wall of the castle, built in 1540; and several indents from Thetford Priory were used to pave a kitchen floor. Some slabs from Eynsham Abbey, indented for early brasses with Lombardic inscriptions, were used to build a mill at Hardwick, and another was re-used for a brass of 1645 at Elsfield.[12] A fine indent, probably from Battle Abbey, was found in a kitchen garden at a farmhouse at Priesthawes, and a fourteenth-century indent from Robertsbridge Abbey is now in the coachhouse of the modern Abbey house. At Hardham Priory, near Pulborough, part of an early indent is in a garden rockery.

Following the dissolution of the monasteries came the seizure of colleges, hospitals, chantries and any other religious or charitable institutions the king could lay his hands on, and brasses from these also were sold and destroyed. When Malling College, near Lewes, was suppressed, it was estimated that twenty-nine 'marbyll stones, wherin werre Images and scrypturs of brasse, the which brasse ys bettyn owtt and stollyn, and the stones moche spoylyd' would be worth 20s. When the material was sold, however, it fetched more than twice the estimate: 'Item of Geffrye Saxbye Merill and other for paving stone . . . xls vid', and 'Rec. for the Brassys, and olde Iron of the belles . . . xiijs iiijd.'[13]

17

The example set by the king in robbing the church was soon followed by the Commons, and between 1540 and 1550 many brasses were torn up and sold either by the churchwardens or by unauthorised iconoclasts. The growing Protestant movement applied the Old Testament denunciations of pagan idols to Christian painting and sculpture, trampling figures of its own Saviour with the same zeal with which Gideon had burnt the pillar of Baal. Iconoclastic preachers would stir up the local population into raiding the parish church and overthrowing the statues, breaking windows, defacing frescoes and burning books. Brasses and tomb sculpture might have been thought innocuous portraits of the reformers themselves, of which there is no lack, but once a mood of destructiveness had settled on the people, they would not have confined themselves to the destruction of wooden and plaster saints and forgone the much more profitable destruction of brazen sinners. Brasses alone among the 'graven images' of medieval churches had a commercial value, and whereas smashing windows and beheading statues might be fun, there was no market for the remains. As a result many churches have been stripped of their brasses while the saints remain undamaged in the windows.

Until 1548 the government still officially disapproved of iconoclasm in any form, and as late as 1547 we find the Privy Council ordering the churchwardens to restore a crucifix they had destroyed in St Martin's, Ironmongers Lane, London. Yet in that year at St Martin's, Leicester, three lots of brasses totalling 9 cwt were sold at 19s per cwt.[14] An Order in Council of 1548 directed the clergy to remove all images and statues of any kind from their churches, and this was followed in 1550 by an 'Act for the abolishing and putting away of divers books and images', which decreed that anyone preserving and failing to destroy any 'images of stone, timber, alabaster or earth, graven, carved or painted' was liable to a fine of 10s, *'Provided* that this act shall not extend to anie Image, or picture set or graven upon anie church . . . onlie for a monu-

18

ment of any King, prince, nobleman or other dead person'.[15] In other words the Act did not require the destruction of brasses, and specifically excluded all monuments of the dead. But once vandalism had been given the royal assent, church-wardens were not going to jib at destroying brasses along with other images.

We hear, for instance, of brasses being sold at 18s per cwt in 1548 from St Thomas's, Salisbury; 310 lb of brass from Wells Cathedral sold for £3 12s 1d in 1549-50; and 81 lb of brass from Thame for 13s 6d in 1550.[16]

It is likely that many of the cathedrals were stripped of brasses at this time; certainly very little can have been left in Wells if so much of its brass was sold. As Macklin said, had the reign of Edward VI continued much longer, we would now have to number our brasses in hundreds rather than thousands.[17]

DESTRUCTION FROM 1553 TO 1642

Of the destruction during Queen Elizabeth's reign, John Weever wrote in 1631:

> Toward the latter end of the raigne of *Henry* the eight, and throughout the whole raigne of *Edward* the sixth, and in the beginning of Queene *Elizabeth,* certaine persons of every County were put in authority to pull downe, and cast out of all Churches, Roodes, graven Images, Shrines with their reliques, to which the ignorant people came flocking in adoration . . . Marbles which covered the dead were digged up, and put to other uses, Tombes hackt and hewne apeeces; Images or representations of the defunct, broken, erazed, cut or dismembred, Inscriptions or Epitaphs, especially if they began with an *orate pro anima,* or concluded with *cuius animae propitietur Deus.* For greedinesse of the brasse, or for that they were thought to bee Antichristian, pulled out from the sepulchres and purloined . . .[18]

This picture of the chaos of the mid-sixteenth century reads

19

more like an account of the Reign of Terror than the reformation of a Christian church under constitutional government. It is confirmed, however, by a decree of 1559, issued personally by Queen Elizabeth, which describes how 'the Churches and places remaine at this present day spoiled, broken, and ruinated' and how frequently parsons and parishioners had unroofed their churches and sold the lead and bells, 'converting the same to their private gaine'. Although the plundering and sacrilege was stopped briefly during the reign of Good Queen Mary, not much repair was done, and iconoclasm broke out again on the accession of the Protestant Elizabeth. Again church brasses were sold, though the Queen did, in the decree mentioned, forbid 'the breaking or defacing of any parcell of any Monument, or Tombe, or Grave, or other Inscription and memory of any person deceased',[19] and also commanded that all monuments already defaced be repaired at the expense of the persons responsible or their heirs. 'These proclamations tooke small effect', Weever says, blaming this on the rise of Puritanism, but there is plenty of evidence that the authorities of the Established Church continued to deface and sell brasses for their own profit throughout the reigns of Elizabeth and her successors. At Tarring in Sussex the accounts for 1580 include 'Item at the taking down of iij paire of brasses',[20] and we hear of the vicar of St Leonard's, Shoreditch, who 'took away the brasses for covetousnesse' about 1600; he afterwards 'went over into Ireland, and there ignominiously ended his dayes'.[21]

By the end of this period most of the cathedrals had been stripped of their brasses. Certainly by 1635, when Lieutenant Hammond toured the country, he found the brasses already lost from Rochester ('dismembred, defac'd and debus'd'), Canterbury ('all much defac'd and obscur'd by time'), Chichester ('the gravings so much raz'd, and the Brasse pick'd out and stolne away'), and Ely ('disarm'd, dislegg'd and beheaded, by some who preferr'd their owne lucre before the Churches adornement').[22] Anthony Wood records that

Dean Duppa of Oxford used old indents to 'plank a sink that conveyed water underground from the pump in the great Quadrangle towards their house of easement, by Trillmill stream'.[23] Indents were evidently popular for drains and watercourses.

Besides condoning, or initiating, straightforward sale and plunder, church authorities cared little about the destruction of brasses by building works: for example, the laying of a new floor in Magdalen College Chapel, Oxford, in 1634 caused havoc among the brasses. This indifference on the part of the authorities led to much petty thieving and burglary, for which religious motives could always be pleaded if anyone was caught. A thief who stole from St Mary's, Oxford, however, was 'taken with some of the brass about him y^t he had stolen away in ye night-time, was set in the public stockes for his punishment with the brass hanging about his neck & afterwards whipt'.[24]

During this period also a certain amount of judicial mutilation took place, only parts of brasses that could be considered 'popish' being removed. There is little dated evidence, but churchwardens' accounts for Yeovil in 1565 say 2d was paid for 'puttynge out of the two pictors vppon the brasse Dexte that the lessuns be reade on'.[25] Less scrupulous wardens would have sold the whole desk, which is all of cast brass and very valuable.

The English, of course, were not the only iconoclasts, for at the same time brasses across the Channel were being damaged just as much. At St Jacques, Bruges, in 1593, for instance, a fine brass was cut up and made into so Catholic an article as a tabernacle.[26]

On the secular side, the Heralds in their Visitations were authorised to remove unregistered coats of arms and merchants' marks displayed illegally on shields, and there is some evidence that they did so on brasses in London churches. Slabs and brasses also continued to be re-used as raw material for new monuments. At Firle, Sussex, John Gage ordered some brasses from the Johnson workshop to be set in slabs that he would provide,[27] and these slabs, which are all old indents, were evidently picked up cheaply; perhaps they were some of the spoils from Lewes or Malling, still unused.

THE CIVIL WAR AND COMMONWEALTH

All authorities writing at any time since 1660 assure us that most of the destruction of brasses was the personal responsibility of Oliver Cromwell, whose greatest delight it was, it would seem, apart from breaking windows. Any church guide, or any romantic writer on old English churches, may be relied on to blame Cromwell for all and every piece of damage to fabric and fittings. In fact, as we have seen, brasses had suffered most severely long before the outbreak of the war. In any case the most destructive phase of the war itself was 1642-4, before Cromwell had become the chief man of affairs.

In any war a captured city is liable to be looted and its buildings damaged by victorious soldiers, and while such sacking is always more shocking in a civil war, there is no evidence to show it was any worse than previous sacks inflicted on conquered English cities. England, however, was unused to such events, and contemporary writers speak with horror and amazement of the ravages of the Parliamentary armies. Bruno Ryves, a Royalist propagandist writing as 'Mercurius Rusticus', describes how the cathedrals were treated during the first phase of the war in 1642, as cities were taken. In each case he speaks of a spontaneous riot of unleashed soldiers breaking whatever they could break and, in particular, destroying books and vestments: for instance, in Canterbury in August 1642 they 'overthrew the Communion table, toare the Velvet-Cloth from before it, defaced the goodly Screene or Tabernacle-worke, violated the Monuments of the dead, spoyled the Organs etc'. On the whole 'violating the monuments of the dead', which Mercurius views with particular horror, seems to have involved knocking noses and hands off carved stone effigies rather than tearing up brasses. At Winchester in December 1642, for example, 'they turne to the Monuments of the dead, some they utterly demolish, others they deface . . . they attempted to deface the Monument of the late Lord Treasurer the Earle of Portland, but being in Brasse, their violence made small impression on it, therefore they leave that, and turne to his Fathers Monument, which being of stone, was more obnoxious to their fury.' Presumably a well-fixed brass could withstand a hammering from drunken soldiers with pole-axes and the ill-organised vandalism of this sort of sack.

Mercurius in fact gives only one definite instance of brasses being torn up and sold: at Peterborough he says, 'not one monument in the Church escaped undefaced, no not of the Pious Benefactors . . . nor those two faire Tombes of Katherine Queen Dowager of Spaine, the Repudiate of King H. 8 [which certainly incorporated a brass] and Mary, albeit Queen of Scots . . . they sold the Brasse they flaid from the graven Stones.' In other churches, as we have seen, the damage had been done long before—as at Chichester, where they 'ran up and downe the Church, with their swords drawne, defacing the Monuments of the dead', or at Rochester, where, surprisingly, 'the multitude, though mad enough, yet were not so mad, nor stood yet so prepar'd to approve such heathenish practices: by this means the Monuments of the dead, which elsewhere they brake up and violated, stood untouched.'[28] Further afield we hear of brasses and coats of arms being defaced in Waterford Cathedral during the Irish campaign, and doubtless there were several other genuine instances of Parliamentary damage to brasses. At York, however, Sir Thomas Fairfax specifically arranged that the Cathedral and churches be spared after the surrender of the city, and the brasses were also spared at Lincoln during the Civil War itself.

On the other side, Anthony Wood, after describing the brasses once existing in New College cloisters, says that most, 'especially those engraven on brass plates, were sacrilegiously conveyed away, when the King's ammunition was reposed therein in the time of the Civil War, an. 1643 and after.'[29] Both sides were guilty of enormities, as in any war, though there is plenty of evidence of sacrilege without too much damage: General Waller used Arundel church as a stable and barracks, yet the brasses survived undamaged until the eighteenth century; St Alban's Abbey was used as a prison, and here too the brasses do not seem to have been damaged; the king used two Oxford churches as prisons, and we hear of indignant complaints that the men burnt pews to keep themselves warm; yet the brasses in St Mary Magdalen's, including a superb scene of the invocation of saints, survived till much later.

As well as damage inflicted by the accidents of war, many brasses were mutilated or destroyed following a repetition of the Act against images. The 1641 'Resolutions on Ecclesiastical Innovations' state 'That all crucifixes, scandalous pictures of any one or more persons of the Trinity, and all images of the Virgin Mary shall be taken away and abolished.'[30] This was followed by an Ordinance of 28 August 1643 repeating the Act of Edward VI almost word for word, and with the same exemption for all monuments of the dead. It does not seem to have led to quite such indiscriminate destruction as before, and it is remarkable how many brasses survive complete save for the 'offensive' parts, where less scrupulous men in the sixteenth century would have destroyed the whole monument.

The most famous record of the carrying out of the Parliamentary instruction is the diary of William Dowsing, who received a warrant from the Earl of Manchester to inspect churches in Suffolk and Cambridgeshire, and to remove 'superstitious pictures and ornaments'.[31] He is referred to by the royalists as 'one who calls himselfe *John Dowsing,* and by vertue of a pretended Commission goes about the Country like a Bedlam, breaking glosse windowes . . .'[32] His diary shows that he destroyed 'pictures' in large numbers, but it has been

24

pointed out by F. J. Varley that these were not windows but
icons of wood, canvas or even paper, which had become very
popular under Laud.[33] Occasionally the diary does specify
windows, and it also mentions angels in hammerbeam roofs
and other carvings. Dowsing's interest in brasses seems to
have centred exclusively on inscriptions; he records the removal of inscriptions reading *'orate pro anima',* but very
often the figures and even a Trinity (at Orford) remain to this
day. He mentions a few Trinities, saints or scrolls, as at
Glensford, 26 February 1643-4, 'one of God the Father, a
picture of the Holy Ghost, in brass', and at St Benet's, Cambridge, where the Billingford brass was deprived of its inscription, scroll and Virgin. He claims to have removed some fifty-
eight inscriptions from Cambridgeshire, and at least 198 from
Suffolk, usually claiming a fee of one noble or 6s 8d from each
church. Only once does he seem to have investigated the value
of the metal, and that was at Wetherden, 5 February 1643-4,
where he took up 'nineteen superstitious inscriptions that
weighed sixty-five pounds', and on the whole he does not seem
to have made any profit on the commission above his 'fee'.
One inscription survived him, at Mettfield, Suffolk; he notes
it as being to John and Isabel Jermy, 1504, and records that
'Mr Jermin, the gentleman in the town, refused to take up the
inscription, as the churchwardens informed'.

In at least two instances Suffolk churchwardens anticipated
Dowsing's coming by pulling up and presumably selling the
brasses beforehand. At St Clement's, Ipswich, 30 January
1643-4, 'They four days beforehand had beaten up divers
superstitious inscriptions'; and at Walberswick the churchwardens' accounts record the payment of 1s 'to others for
taking up the brasses of gravestones befor the officer Dowson
came' as well as the 6s 'April 8th, paid to master Dowson
that came with the troopers to our church, about the taking
down of images, and brasses off stones'. Dowsing removed
eight inscriptions, but obviously left the figures as usual, for
there was still enough brass left nine months later for the

accounts to record, 'Re. this 6th January 1644 [ie 1645] from out of the church, 40 pounds weyght of brasse, at threepence halfpenny per pound £0 . . 11 . . 8.'[34]

Elsewhere the churchwardens' accounts show that the Parliamentary instructions and the general confusion of the times were again made an excuse for the sale of brasses: at St Margaret's, Westminster in 1644, for instance, they record 'Item. for 29 pound of fine brasse at 4d a pound, and 96 pound of coarse brasse at 3d a pound taken off from sundrie tombestones in the church. £1:13:6.'[35] (One feels they deserved to be cheated of the missing 2d!) And again, in other places the wardens followed the letter of the law more strictly and merely erased offending words or symbols. In All Hallows by the Tower, London, the vestry paid 16s in 1643 'to erase the superstitious letters'; it was done very neatly and efficiently, as may be seen to this day. Many other inscriptions were censored of 'Catholic' phrases, and occasionally emblems or images were defaced, as at St Patrick's Cathedral where the initials of the person commemorated on the brass have been carefully engraved across the Trinity, and a wheel substituted for the Father's head.[36]

It is difficult after three centuries to understand the motives that prompted such rigid censorship. Plundering by soldiers is inevitable, and sale for private gain is understandable, but it seems odd to go around with mallet and chisel solemnly removing all tangible evidence that England had once been Catholic. The reformers seemed unable to distinguish between the Christian's use of an image to remind him of God or the saints and to concentrate his mind in prayer, and the pagan's totem-worship of the thing itself. They objected, too, to any plea on brasses that souls should be prayed for, or any invocation of saints. At a time when religious conformity was made a matter of national security, to pray for the dead was thought tantamount to supporting a Spanish invasion.

After the end of the Civil War, during the Commonwealth, there seems to have been little desecration or damage.

Anthony Wood notices only two instances of brasses in Oxford being lost during the Interregnum, both in his own college of Merton and both cases of petty thieving by workmen brought in for repairs and repainting.[37] A few more churchwardens' accounts itemise the sale of brasses, as at Christchurch in Hampshire, where an indent seems to have been sold in 1657.[38] On the whole, however, the storm seems to have died down, which makes the isolated cases of York and Lincoln all the more remarkable.

The brasses in both these cathedrals, as we have seen, survived the Civil War, but during the following peace nearly all of them were lost. In York about 1650 'all the brasse which was taken of the gravestones' was 'sold by Mr Dossey by order from the Lord Mayor'.[39] Some brasses survived at York, as a few do even now, but at Lincoln there seems to have been a clean sweep. John Evelyn records in his diary (19 August 1654) that 'the Souldiers had lately knocked off all or most of the Brasses which were on the Gravestones, so as few Inscriptions were left. They told us they went in with axes & hammers, & shut themselves in till they had rent & torne of some barges full of Mettal; not sparing the monuments of the dead, so helish an avarice possess'd them.' In 1718 207 indents were counted; we know there were originally nine brasses of bishops, a cast effigy of a queen, and at least eight thirteenth-century brasses. The despoliation of Lincoln is the largest single act of destruction recorded, and it is this which is usually quoted as an example of the infamy of Cromwell. It was, of course, nothing to do with Cromwell, any more than the theft at Oulton in 1857 was the work of Queen Victoria, but almost certainly the work of one of the officers of the garrison.

The Civil War and Commonwealth period was indeed one of destruction and plunder, but to nothing like the extent normally believed. Both royalists and Parliamentarians must have destroyed brasses in the course of the fighting, but since all subsequent historians have tended to favour the eventual

27

victors, we get a rather biased view of events. Anthony Wood records an inscription in All Saints', Oxford, about 1660 that was mutilated by the time Dingley saw it in about 1680, and the latter has no hesitation in referring to it as 'the brass stolen away by rebells'. Even as late as 1880 a popular guidebook to Oxford quotes the churchwardens' accounts of All Saints' as authority that the brasses 'were torn from their position during the Commonwealth and sold to a Mr Payne for £2-1s'-though the accounts clearly date this sale to 1701![40]

LOSSES BETWEEN 1660 AND 1833

From the mid-seventeenth century onwards our information on the destruction and preservation of brasses becomes progressively more complete. Antiquaries increasingly recorded monuments and brasses, and often gave details on how and when they were lost. Throughout the eighteenth century antiquarianism became more popular, nearly every county finding a historian who collected epitaphs and bewailed their destruction.

Normally churchwardens and incumbents took not the slightest interest in brasses and monuments as such; it was only eccentrics like the antiquaries who bothered about them. Wardens frequently made no scruple at selling off their brasses to travelling tinkers simply as an easy way of raising money, without even the excuse of religious iconoclasm. Cotman records that the splendid brasses at Ingham in Norfolk were sold in 1800 'as old metal, and it was commonly reported by whom they were sold and bought; but nobody sought to recover them: neither the minister nor churchwardens cared for any of these things.'[41] We know of two authorised sales of brasses at King's Lynn, in 1742 and 1746. At Upminster 'the sepulchral brass of Roger Deincourt, who died, according to the epitaph given by Weever, in 1455, was sold some time ago to an itinerant tinker',[42] and at Saffron Walden the brasses that had survived the purge of 1643 were taken up during repewing in 1804 and sold to a brazier named Peachey, though some were recovered.[43] The brasses at Wingfield in Suffolk that Gough recorded about 1760 were 'since converted into money by one of the churchwardens', though Manning more picturesquely says they 'are said to have been *borrowed* by a gentleman who called for them in his gig and carried them off!'[44] Again we find parallels to this behaviour on the Continent, where the magnificent royal brasses at Ribe and Roskilde in Denmark were sold to a coppersmith, and a large collection from St Walburghe's at Bruges was sold in 1777.

Churchwardens would also make use of the metal for their own purposes. At Luton in the mid-eighteenth century several brasses were melted down and cast as a chandelier, and at Meopham in Kent 'some of the bells of the church being to be new cast, and there being wanting a sufficient quantity of metal to do it, some persons . . . tore off all the brass inscriptions from the stones in the church . . . and threw them into the melted metal, to add to its quantity for casting the bells.'[45] An inscription at York was converted into a weathercock soon after the Restoration. A more unusual appropriation occurred at Bowers Gifford in Essex, where the churchwarden took the brass and it was found 'serving the purpose of covering some holes in the shelf of a storeroom. Shortly afterwards the end of the sword fell a victim to a boy's efforts to possess himself of so desirable a weapon.' The brass was later given to 'a gentleman resident in Billericay' from whom it was eventually recovered for the church.[46]

A great many brasses were lost in the eighteenth century by simple neglect during building work, being either picked up by petty thieves or buried under rubble. When the west front of Hereford Cathedral collapsed in 1786, some 2 tonnes of brass are said to have been sent to a brazier, though Gough (who seems to have acquired them) merely says 'several capital brasses . . . were torn up by the rapacity of the workmen before the vergers could prevent them'.[47] At Durham the brasses in the chapter-house were just as wantonly destroyed in 1799: 'The building was held to be too large, and doomed to destruction, for no other purpose than to make a comfortable room. Accordingly a man was suspended by tackle above the groining and knocked out the keystone, when the whole fell, and crushed the paved floor, rich with gravestones, and brasses of the Bishops and Priors, not one of which had been copied or preserved in any form.'[48]

Most of the brasses of St George's, Windsor, were lost when the chapel was repaved in 1805. John Carter wrote sarcastically to the *Gentleman's Magazine:*

> The pavement has been re-laid, and in the new way: that got rid of was remarkable for the number and variety of sepulchral stones inlaid with highly curious and valuable brasses, rendering a choice display of historical and characteristic memorials. . . what became of these relics I shall not set out to declare: why need I express my concern for their loss other than as an antiquary? No line of ancestry is broken to which I am a distant branch-what is it to me who were the antient Religious of the pile, or how their robes adorned them; such members being out of recollection, and such vestments useless.[49]

The attitude Carter pillories must have been prevalent among the church authorities of the time, since in almost every known case of church repair or rebuilding during the eighteenth century, the brasses were simply thrown away or sold without thought. The brasses at Arundel that escaped untouched when General Waller stabled his horses on top of them, for instance, were purloined by workmen after the fall of the roof in 1782. Many brasses were sold off during the rebuilding of the church of Leatheringham in Suffolk; Nichols writes of a brass 'originally fixed in the wall, but which, after the demolition of the church, accompanied the sale of the old materials, and is now in my possession'.[50] In Oxford in 1814 a very interesting late seventeenth-century brass was lost when St Ebbe's church was rebuilt (see Plate 4b), several more probably in 1820 when St Martin's was rebuilt; and after the church of All Saints' collapsed in 1699-1700, the church-wardens' accounts record, 'Item, Rec'd of Mr Payne for Brass . . . 02:01:00', though, to do them justice, the church-wardens did have the decency to set up tablets to commem-orate those to whom the brasses had belonged.[51]

Where churches were completely destroyed, the brasses seem invariably to have been destroyed as well. At Dunwich in Suffolk and Reculver in Kent fine churches were pulled to pieces in advance of an encroaching sea (quite unnecessarily at Reculver, where the towers still stand high and dry), and the brasses were abandoned and eventually stolen. Reculver is described in a series of angry letters to the *Gentleman's Magazine*: by summer 1810 the church 'is fast hastening to ruin-some beautiful brasses have been stolen within these two months from tombstones in the chancel'.[52] The chapel of Eythrope in Buckinghamshire was demolished in 1738 so that the stone could be used for building a bridge, and a large brass was simply buried under rubble till it was discovered in 1901. Probably the worst loss of this kind occurred at St Alkmund's, Shrewsbury, where the brasses were sold off by weight when the church was demolished-a particularly tanta-lising loss, since surviving drawings show that the brasses were fine and unusual specimens.

More annoying perhaps is the way in which many brasses were slowly picked to pieces over a long period. Presumably parts worked loose and no one bothered to secure them, so they were picked up by thieves or swept up with the dust. The dismemberment of a fine brass at Chieveley, Berkshire, in this way was recorded by Henry Hinton, who wrote in 1812 that 'The Inscriptions & Arms are lost, the Effigie remains', and in 1815 that 'The effigie remained till a few years past, [but] only one coat of arms now remains'.[53]

Some thefts seem to have been purely mischievous, as with a brass in Peel Cathedral, which was stolen about 1798 and found in 1844 at the bottom of a well in Peel Castle. Elsewhere churches were broken into at night and brasses stolen, as at Thatcham, Berkshire. In at least one case, at Lutterworth in Leicestershire, the thieves were caught; Haines records that 'Some of these brasses were stolen about 1836 by a man who was transported for the offence. No II was preserved by Mr Hilpack, the parish clerk'.[54] Sometimes parish clerks or sextons themselves plundered the church for their own profit, as did the clerk of Methwold, who sold the brass in 1680 to a travelling tinker, from whom only fragments could be recovered, or the sexton of King's Lynn who, according to Albert Way, sold a great Flemish brass for 5s in 1800 and is said to have hanged himself in remorse, though other sources say this brass was sold by order of the churchwardens several years before.[55] Sometimes the local squire intervened and appropriated brasses on the grounds that they commemorated his ancestors, as at Portslade in Sussex, though sometimes he wanted the slabs simply as paving. Gough records an unnamed church in Suffolk, 'a church where all the monuments of former lords of the manor were sacrificed to the vanity of the present proprietor, who having no train of ancestry to boast of, could not bear the memorials of those who had. One brass only escaped, which I have engraved.'[56]

In addition to losses through theft, several of the antiquaries themselves were appropriating brasses. Often, of course, they took the brasses only to save them from the melting pot: Wood seems to have walked off with several from Merton, Gough and Nichols with brasses from Hereford and elsewhere, and Stukeley with a curious double palimpsest from Great Stukeley. Very few of the brasses they took, however, were eventually preserved, as, except for two plates which Gough gave to the Bodleian, all are now lost. Other antiquaries did not wait for an excuse to collect brasses, as at Stanford, Leicestershire where four quite interesting brasses were 'removed by Sir Thomas Cave to Stanford Hall, for their better preservation, but have unfortunately all been lost.[57] The brasses from Little Chesterford, Essex, loose in the church in 1744, were seen in 1781 'inlaid in the passage of the house of Mr Rich. Reynolds, Market Hill, Cambridge': some of them have since arrived in the Cambridge Museum.[58] An interesting example of the reversal of the normal role of rapacious sexton and zealous antiquarian is preserved in a letter in Hinton's MSS in the Bodleian:

Copy of a letter verbatim et literatim from a Ch. warden of Walton upon Thames to a Mr — in answer to a letter in which Mr W— requested leave to take out of the church a brass monumental plate in order to make a drawing of it. "Sir. I am very sorry I cant be agreeable as to what you ax me to do! but by the cannon Law nobody must not presume to take nothing out of the Church especialy the Sakred Utensils upon pain of Blasphemy, I must therefore refuse you the brass monumental Tom Stone which you desired but you are welcum to cum into the church and Draw it about as much as you please."[59]

THE AGE OF RESTORATIONS

Ritualism and the inauguration of the Oxford Movement in 1833 led to an increasing interest in church buildings and fittings. This revival not only spawned the first great wave of brass-rubbers and led to the first books devoted solely to brasses, but also led to a disastrous programme of church restoration that deprived English churches of much of their character and destroyed or spoilt hundreds of brasses.

The principle behind the nineteenth-century restorations was that Christian art and architecture had reached its most perfect form in the thirteenth century, in the 'Middle Pointed' style; any earlier style was semi-barbaric and any later style was decadent or heathen. This attitude was applied, and by an astonishing number of writers is still applied, to monumental brasses: as Creeny wrote, 'The decay of monumental engraving as a special art keeps pace with the classic revival'.[60] A large number of very interesting Renaissance or Baroque brasses were probably thrown away as being out of keeping with a 're-Gothicised' church. The work of restoration itself was responsible for the destruction of many brasses, as altar-tombs and monuments were swept away with box-pews, galleries and anything else that might obstruct the Oxford Movement. Frequently churches were found to be in a bad state of repair after some three centuries of neglect, and so were demolished completely and the site cleared before rebuilding. Any surviving brasses were usually mixed up with each other and wrongly set in new stones, while the indents preserving the original arrangement were buried or broken up: the results may be seen at Taplow, Buckinghamshire; St Peter le Bailey, Oxford; St Giles, Camberwell; Sonning, Berkshire; Northfleet, Kent and many others. The last is a particularly bad example, since of thirteen brasses only three survive, and those are badly mutilated. The finest of these, Peter de Lacy, 1375, originally had a canopied effigy within a marginal fillet, but the canopy was thrown away (part of it is now in the British Museum), and the figure relaid within the marginal inscription cut down to keep the proportions correct. Of the other brasses, it is said that fragments survive in the slabs, which were concreted over.[61]

In nearly every church where restoration took place indents were heedlessly destroyed or buried, for it often took a specialist to detect and appreciate them, and architects usually left far too much to the discretion of the local builder. Dunkin records how two indents in Bodmin church were used as a base for mixing lime, and though the vicar and Dunkin's correspondent carefully cleaned them, they found them a few weeks later set up in the trench round the church walls.[62] Indents are still frequently found in churchyards whither they were once banished by restorers, as at West Grinstead, Sussex; St Lawrence, Reading; or St Martin's, Leicester; or even laid in the roadside verge outside the churchyard, as at Woolbeding, Sussex.

Not only indents but brasses themselves were often thrown away or stolen in large numbers from churches where com-

paratively little restoration took place. Usually the laying of
an underfloor heating system and a new paving of encaustic
tiles led to the brasses being lifted, and once loose they were
very often appropriated by the workmen. The fine fourteenth-
century brass at Marcham, Berkshire, known to us from
Hinton's rubbing, was sold by a workman in 1837 for 5s (see
Plate 1b).[63] At Toddington, Bedfordshire, the brasses were
found in 1881 heaped up among builders' rubble.[64] At Maw-
gan in Pyder, Cornwall, the brasses were all torn up-only
three effigies were allowed to remain in the church-and scattered up and down England, whence they have only recently
been collected. St Mary Magdalen's, Canterbury, lost five
brasses in 1871, though, curiously, the indents were preserved
and moved to a neighbouring church.[65] At Carlton, Suffolk,
in 1878 a figure brass was thrown out and the indent destroyed; the brass was bought by a Mr Stanley, however, from
whom it found its way back to the church in 1892. Winchester
College lost all the brasses from the chapel in 1875, when they
were replaced with facsimiles made from old rubbings. The
list of brasses lost, stolen, thrown away or missing without
trace because of nineteenth-century restorations is endless.
One only need compare Haines' list of 1861 with Mill
Stephenson's list of 1926 to appreciate the extent of the destruction.

Surviving brasses were sometimes treated in strange and
barbaric ways. Perhaps the most perverse of 'restorers' were
the vicar and curate of Playford, Suffolk, who, in December
or January 1837-8, 'went to the church with tools, and with
their own hands ripped off the canopy which covered the
figure, and the whole of the inscription which surrounded it.
It appeared . . . that they imagined the commercial value of
the few ounces of metal thus torn off to be so great that it
would enable them to mount the figure in a more splendid
manner.'[66] At Streatley, Berkshire, a foot of concrete was
poured over the brass, which remains entombed to this day.
At Warkworth, Northamptonshire, Haines tells us that half

the brasses were buried under a heavy stone, presumably lest their ghosts walk. At Corpus Christi College, Oxford, two mural brasses were imprisoned behind the panelling or organ, and the shroud brass on the floor was for a long time covered with a sheet of lead, the figure being visible only through an opening. At St Mary the Virgin, Oxford, the most interesting brass was hoisted high up over the tower arch, where it can still be seen with a good pair of field glasses! At Stadhampton in Oxfordshire the brasses, which comprised two family groups, with inscriptions, were rearranged: the two husbands were set together, with the larger inscription; the two wives together, with the second inscription, upside down; the children were tastefully arranged between them; and all were cemented on to a rough wall.[67]

Even where brasses were appreciated and cared for, they were too often separated from their stone slabs, to which they should have been securely fixed. Many were kept by incumbents or churchwardens in their homes, and others were locked in a chest or left lying in the vestry. Mill Stephenson records brasses stored in the vicarage, the church chest, or even the vestry coal hole, and often the *Appendix* of 1938 has to add that they are no longer to be found. Often local antiquarians or gentry 'took brasses into safe keeping' after they had been loosened during restoration. Occasionally brasses found their way back into churches, but the list is full of notes on those that disappeared into private hands in the late nineteenth century and have since vanished, for on the death of the original possessor they were usually sold with his effects. Interesting brasses discovered at Arthuret, Cumberland, and St Non's chapel near St David's (both in areas very short of brasses) were taken into private possession; that from Arthuret has since been returned to the church, but the oldest brass in Wales is still missing. Two brasses from Chalfont St Peter, Buckinghamshire, were removed from the church about 1860, and by 1912 had got to Newark, whence they disappeared about 1920. A brass from Magdalen College,

Oxford, was sold with the library of a Fellow who had presumably appropriated it, and was only recovered when it was bought back by Haines.[68] Another example connected with Haines was an inscription from Hook Norton, Oxfordshire, which 'was sent by one of the churchwardens (a farmer) to a blacksmith at Bloxham, for him to mend his plough with. The blacksmith, not being accustomed to work with such materials, sent word to this guardian of the church and its sacred relics that it was of no use, because it was not iron. It was then thrown aside in his shop, from whence it got into the hands of a general dealer in Banbury, of whom Mr Faulkner bought it for 2s.' Faulkner was a friend of Haines and an antiquary, but nevertheless the brass has never been seen since.[69]

Again in this century we find unscrupulous antiquaries attempting to 'collect' brasses. The Vicar of Odiham wrote to the Cambridge University Association of Brass Collectors (whose choice of name lost them much goodwill): 'All the seven brasses are in good order. They were loose for a long time in the old chest, and were collected by me in 1867 and affixed to the wall, as I found that a few archaeological gentlemen had offered our sexton money for them, which he refused.'[70] At Aveley in Essex half a brass inscription was lost in 1856 but dug up at Romford in 1878 and was taken back to the church in 1892; there it was compared with the half in the slab, which was promptly torn up by 'two clerical gentlemen, assisted by the church clerk'. The owner of the previously loose half protested that the whole should be refixed in its proper place, but on the refusal of the vicar to allow this he deposited the plate in Colchester Museum till it could be repaired and refixed.[71]

As well as these documented losses, there was a steady trickle of common thefts, whose motive probably changed gradually from a simple desire to acquire valuable metal to the wish to possess something of antiquarian or collecting value. Stolen brasses in early Victorian times were probably quickly passed on to the brazier, but most of the brasses stolen after the increase of popular interest probably still exist in some private collection or lie unrecognised in a museum. Unfortunately, the brazier almost certainly swallowed up the three serious losses of 1856-7: from Cowthorpe in Yorkshire, Okeover in Staffordshire, and Oulton in Suffolk. The first was a very important brass to a judge and wife holding a model church, the second an impressive palimpsest that was severely damaged by the thieves, and the third the brass of a priest, usually dated c1310 and certainly one of the earliest in England, which was the greatest loss to English brasses since they have been studied. Other stolen brasses have been recovered, like the Washington brasses at Sulgrave, Northamptonshire, taken in 1889; and there was a near theft in 1892 at Swaffham Prior, Cambridgeshire, where 'the sexton, we understand, was just in time to prevent the thief from removing William Wake's brass'.[72]

Small pieces of brass continued to be stolen, as at all periods, and we frequently find that early nineteenth-century rubbings or drawings show brasses substantially more complete than they were by the end of the century. Shields, heads, scrolls and the like continued to disappear, despite the increasing awareness of the clergy and public of the importance of antiquities. These included the very curious and early shield from Stanton Harcourt, Oxfordshire, said to date from 1293, and stolen about 1860. An inscription from Royston, Hertfordshire, which was loose in the church in 1880 was found in 1891 being used locally as a door-scraper.

Nineteenth-century losses are better documented than before, and a substantial proportion of them can be made good by referring to old rubbings, but many brasses must have been lost without record. Often they were taken by the very people who claimed to have an interest in ecclesiastical art.

LOSSES AFTER 1914

People are often surprised to hear that brasses are still being lost, and at an alarming rate. In fact a number of important brasses have been lost this century, and there is no reason to suppose that the trend is declining. Obviously this period is completely documented, and every brass lost recently is well recorded in rubbings. The losses to scholarship, therefore, are not so great, though they loom large as thefts of known and counted objects.

The largest single cause was, of course, the bombing and shelling during the two World Wars. Rather surprisingly, little damage was done during 1914-18, even in Flanders. At Ypres the brasses seem to have survived undamaged, though Dr Cameron's list contains a note about a brass at Nieuport on the Flemish coast that was picked out of the ruins by a British soldier returning on leave and 'reappeared in 1927 in use as a fire screen in a cottage near London'. It was returned to Nieuport just in time to be destroyed utterly in 1940. Between 1939 and 1945, however, especially in Eastern Europe, appalling damage was done. Several fine brasses were destroyed or taken by looters during the destruction of cities like Gdańsk (Danzig), Poznań , Wrocław (Breslau) or Lübeck. Others were picked apart by soldiers, like the splendid series at Lubiaz near Wrocław, damaged by Soviet soldiers billeted in the Abbey. Nevertheless brasses were amazingly durable, and in some cases survived when churches were reduced to rubble, as at Braniewo (Braunsberg) in Poland, where a very fine brass that was picked up in twenty-five pieces has now been repaired and is on show in Olsztyn Museum.

In England war damage was relatively light. Brasses survived in several churches that were burnt out, as at Little Horkesley, Essex; the Temple Church, Bristol; All Hallows, Barking, London; Lydd, Kent; and Heigham, Norfolk. Brasses were destroyed at Swansea, Coventry and some

London churches, but the most serious losses were of indents, which are much more vulnerable to blast and less likely to be salvaged. About forty were lost in the Austin Friars' church, London.

Worse than the bombing was the plundering that followed it. For the rest of the war, and often for years afterwards, the burnt-out churches lay open to petty thieves and vandals. At All Hallows, Barking, the brasses were protected with a layer of asphalt and all survived, but several were stolen from ruins elsewhere. A unique group of children including an abbot in full pontificals was stolen from Wendon Lofts, Essex, in 1940, a seventeenth-century family group from St James's, Dover; and a civilian from Lydd, Kent. At Pakefield, Suffolk, 'while the church lay derelict everything that could be taken away was stolen; even a brass to a boy (Manners Sutton) was wrenched from the pillar to which it was attached'.[73]

Similar effects were produced by accidental fires, which destroyed churches such as Eaton Socon and Biggleswade, Bedfordshire; Hackney, Middlesex; and Upper Hardres, Kent. In some, as at Upper Hardres, the brasses survived and were lodged in the local museum till the church could be rebuilt. At Eaton Socon, however, one brass was completely destroyed, and another shrivelled up, the head having melted off it. In Biggleswade, on the other hand, the fire led to the discovery of the indent from which the curious brass of John Ruding had long been sundered, and the opportunity was taken to collect and relay the scattered fragments of the brass.

In other churches that have been restored and rebuilt brasses are endangered even now, and there are still examples of indents being destroyed during repairs. The brasses at Prestwold, Leicestershire, vanished when the church was rebuilt in 1930, and those at Lockington in the same county were pulled up and the stones destroyed about 1950. At Chinnor, Oxfordshire, all the brasses were ripped up and screwed to the chancel walls in 1935, but corrosion from the lime plaster has resulted and the plates are constantly coming loose through having no firm hold, and, furthermore, the walls are hideously disfigured by the tape used by brass-rubbers. Yet this act, which also involved flooding the indents with cement, was defended by W. J. Gawthorpe on the grounds that it would save the brasses from being walked on.[74] Similarly the brasses at Magdalen College, Oxford, which had been carefully (if a little inaccurately) relaid at the expense of one of the Fellows in 1911, have all been torn up and screwed to the wall with large disfiguring screws in the last 20 years; some parts arc now upside down, and others lost. Even more recently at least two indents have vanished during the repairs to Chichester Cathedral, and another, which the author noticed outside St Andrew's church in the same city in 1970, was gone a year later. Apparently also in the last two years some incumbents have been pulling up their brasses to hide them from brass-rubbers—a senseless act of vandalism which will almost inevitably lead to the destruction of their indents, and quite possibly to the loss of the brasses themselves.

Redundant churches, of course, are a problem of our age, and the future of their brasses must be in doubt. Sometimes the brasses are moved to neighbouring churches or museums, but as a church has to be left empty for years before it can be declared redundant, vandalism is frequent. At Milland in Sussex the old chapel has most shamefully been allowed to fall into ruin, and at least one of its brasses has been stolen. At Newton by Geddington, Northamptonshire, a brass was stolen by some boys, who apparently hid it in a cave among old iron-workings, where it slipped deeper and was lost.[75] An earlier redundancy was Llanwarne in Herefordshire, where the church was in ruins by 1936; and the brass was kept in the vicarage then, but by 1974 it had gone.

Finally the tale of common thefts is by no means over. Since World War II brasses have been stolen from Ashtead, Compton and Kingston, Surrey; Stoke by Nayland and Polstead, Suffolk; Packington, Leicestershire; Wrotham, Kent;

Great Anwell, Hertfordshire; Clavering, Essex; Sedgefield, Durham; Wing, Buckinghamshire and Wymington, Bedfordshire. Some few have been recovered: at Wrotham they were quietly put back in the pulpit at night, the Suffolk brasses were found by the police, the Clavering brasses were barely saved from a London saleroom, and the head of the knight at Wymington was rescued by a brass-rubber who accosted the thieves. The early lady from Sedgefield was found in the autumn of 1974 nailed to the wall of a pub among the horse brasses. The others are probably not destroyed, and may well turn up eventually in private collections or salerooms.

Notes to this chapter appear on page 185

3

INDENTS

The fair marble which acts the second part of Niobe, weeping
for many figures of Brass which it hath lately forgone (Gunton)

The most common evidence for a lost brass is of course the
indent, matrix or casement remaining after the brass has been
removed, and it is on these that we are to a large extent dependent for our reconstructions of what has been destroyed. The
evidence of an indent comes from the normal method by
which most English and many Continental brasses were made
and fixed: the figures, canopies, shields, inscriptions, and
other parts were engraved on separate pieces of plate cut to
the required outlines and sunk into the stone so that the surface of brass and stone would be level, and, when the brass
was removed, the outlines were perfectly preserved. Manning
likens an indent to a negative fossil. On the earlier brasses
metal was used very sparingly and canopies in particular were
cut and pierced into almost lace-like shapes, all of which left
their impressions in the stone. Inscriptions made up of letters
separately cast in brass were let into individual indents, from
which the inscription can usually be read. Many early brasses
can be reconstructed almost entirely from their indents. Later
brasses tended to be smaller, with less cut-out work; the space
between a man's legs, for instance, came to be cross-hatched
rather than cut away, and outlines eventually become almost
square. Real quadrangular plates, of course, leave only a rec-

tangular indent that tells us very little, though it is usually possible to guess at its approximate date or origin from the type of stone or method of fixing. Indents in good condition often retain some of the pitch used for bedding the brass, and nearly always the lead plugs and brass rivets that held the plates down (Plates 1a, 2a, 2b).

THE SURVIVING INDENTS

The vast majority of surviving indents naturally remain in the churches to which they belong. Many are still in their original positions, though perhaps the majority have been shifted or placed together at some time during the constant upheavals necessary when a church is being used for intra-mural burial. All the surviving indents from Christ Church, Oxford, have been concentrated in two parallel side aisles, including one that must originally have been mural and two that were broken in the process and incorrectly reset. In All Saints' Church in the same city the vestry of the new church built in 1707 was completely paved with indents salvaged from the medieval church. Paving stone has always been expensive, and we find indents frequently re-used to pave less prominent parts of churches, such as vestries or north porches, when the nave and chancel from which they come have been repaved. It is unlikely that indents were often turned upside down for paving, since the undersides were never smoothed and would have made a more uneven floor than the indented sides, though occasionally we find that old indents have been cut up and smoothed down for paving, as at York Minster. In All Saints', Oxford the bottom step of the tower stair has been cut out of an indent, though it retains only a single lead plug to show what it is.

Very occasionally indents have been raised up against a wall to keep them from being walked on, as at Freshwater, Isle of Wight, where the indents have been painted black in contrast to the surrounding stone. They are more often

banished to churchyards, either laid as paths, as again at All
Saints', at Great Chart, Kent, and Midhurst, Sussex, or as
revetting for the drainage trench round the walls, as at Ease-
bourne and Fishbourne, Sussex. Churchyards tend to be used
as dumping grounds for unwanted monuments, and indents
can be found lying loose in the grass. A whole stack were
found in 1951 in the churchyard at St Martin's, Leicester,
where they had lain since the restoration in 1867. At West
Grinstead, Sussex, a fine canopied indent is lying in three
pieces on the less frequented side of the church, where it
escaped notice until recently (Fig 30). Only a few years ago a
very well preserved little indent was moved out of Iffley
Church, Oxfordshire, and propped against a wall, where it
remains in danger of frost damage if nothing else (see Plate
1a). Indents in churchyards are rarely well-preserved, since
frost, moss and ivy take over those that do not lie in the path
of the congregation.

Slabs occasionally drift even further away from their
churches, usually after they have been carted away by a
builder and used for lay purposes. Obviously slabs from
monastic churches were so treated, as already described
Slabs seem frequently to have been adapted for lining drains
or sewers, and we hear of them being so used at Stoke
Gurney, Somerset, and Durham and Worcester Cathedrals,
as well as at Oxford and Nonsuch Palace (already mentioned).
We also hear of them being used, more domestically, for a
garden path (since destroyed) at Geddington, Northamptonshire. One indent from the deserted chapel at Quarrendon,
Buckinghamshire, was re-used as a cottage hearthstone, and
another as part of a cellar floor in a nearby farmhouse.[1]

Indents are occasionally found by archaeological excavation on the site of monastic churches, or churches of deserted
medieval villages. They may be seen still exposed in several of
the great Yorkshire abbeys, such as Byland, Fountains or
Jervaulx. However, indents are rarely found on urban church
sites, for there they would have been plundered for paving.

More common are loose Lombardic letters from early inscriptions, which have been found at Glastonbury, Bardney, Byland, Basingwerk and Dale Abbeys; at the Greyfriars in London and Oxford; and at the Oxford Blackfriars. Without their slabs, of course, their arrangement is unknown, and they can tell us nothing except that such early brasses existed, though a valiant effort was made to connect the letters R and A from Oxford Greyfriars with Roger Bacon. Occasionally also loose rivets are found, as are lead plugs, and scraps of Purbeck marble that may be the remains of indents.

The condition of indents varies immensely, from the clarity of sharp-edged outlines, as at Iffley (Plate 1a), to the obscurity of a completely smooth surface on which the brass is identifiable only by the rivets or plugs. Most are somewhat worn, as they are usually made of Purbeck marble or a similar fossiliferous limestone, which flakes very easily. Frequently the surface is perished but the outline is preserved by the chiselling round the bottom of the indent, though often only a gently rounded hollow remains, giving little clue as to where the exact edge was (see Plates 2a, 2b). A few indents have been preserved by carefully filling the original outlines with coloured cement, as on the tomb of Bishop Arundel at Chichester, but far more have been indiscriminately smothered in cement simply to level the surface. A very fine and complicated early indent at Cranbrook, Kent, is now barely recognisable under its cement veil, though it is fortunately preserved in an early nineteenth-century drawing. With care, of course, the cement can always be removed, and while it is there it is at least saving the indent from being worn; so these slabs are not lost forever.

Numerous indents have been appropriated to serve as later memorials, usually by cutting a new inscription across the stone, as in Oxford, where initials and the date 1643 or 1644 were added to many to commemorate those who died during the Civil War in the siege (Fig 3). Others have had tablets of white marble inserted, often obscuring part of the original design, usually in the eighteenth century. Most of the indents in All Saints' and the Cathedral, Oxford, have been so treated.

Closely akin to indents are the curious phenomena known affectionately as 'ghosts'. These were first sighted in the crypt of Canterbury Cathedral, where, in 1951, F. A. Greenhill was able to photograph some thirteen shadowy outlines of brasses that had been fastened to the walls of the undercroft of Henry IV's chantry. The walls had been discoloured unevenly while the brasses were fixed there, and the outlines survived even though the brasses must have been lost since at least 1800. Thus we have records of several lost brasses, including a very fine crosslegged knight, for which neither indents nor documentary evidence survive.[2] There may well be more such 'ghosts', though the only others known are either quite modern, as at Arundel Cathedral, or those left on a wall when brasses were restored to their original slabs, as at Bramshott, Hampshire. The brasses at Bramshott, in fact, had been on the wall for about 100 years, and had left clear impressions behind them. 'Ghosts' are even more fragile and perishable than indents, of course; such disfiguring patches are rarely tolerated for long on a church wall, so any that are found ought to be photographed immediately, in case they are cleared away.

So far no complete survey has been made of indents, and the number in existence is unknown. The Monumental Brass Society is at present engaged in a revision of the list of brasses, and the new list will also include indents, but this is a long and slow task and will probably take many years. Some areas or counties have been completely surveyed, and many individual churches have been adequately covered, but for much of the country we have to rely on approximations and guesses. From the figures available, however, it is clear that there is no proportional relation between surviving brasses and surviving indents. In East Sussex, for instance, there are only about forty indents and 173 surviving brasses, whereas in

Huntingdonshire there are thirty-four indents and only twenty-eight brasses. Within individual churches the results vary even more.

Usually the critical factor seems to be whether and to what extent a church has been repaved. Some rich parishes have been able to repave completely, and have lost all their indents, whereas others had to keep the slabs for use as paving. In Oxford, for example, the wealthy colleges and parishes such as Magdalen and New College, or St Aldate's church, have lost nearly all their indents, but poorer parishes like All Saints' have preserved them. However, in the Cathedral there are twenty-four indents, and in St Mary's, the University church, there are fifteen (compared to thirteen and seven surviving [mostly late] brasses respectively), and this high rate of survival can certainly not be explained simply by lack of funds for repaving.[3]

Looking at the results of surveys in large churches and cathedrals throughout the country, we find the same sort of inconsistency. St Alban's Abbey contained forty-eight indents when it was surveyed in 1899,[4] while Durham has only eleven. At Chichester thirty-five indents survive in the nave and aisles, but we have drawings of about fourteen more that were lost when the choir was repaved in 1861.[5] Gloucester, on the other hand, has only seven or eight. There is no reason to suppose that the two southern cathedrals were very different in their original number of brasses, though probably the remoter Durham never had quite so many. It must very largely be chance that has left St Alban's and Chichester with so many, and Gloucester with so few. We know that several indents were destroyed in 1741 in Gloucester, and it must be presumed that many more have vanished without trace.

A church that appears to have retained its entire original floor is St Botolph's, Boston, which has the most remarkable collection of slabs in the country. The list of surviving brasses totals twenty-five but of these only three pre-Reformation brasses are at all complete. In contrast, there are sixty-one

Plate 1 Indent in good condition Iffley, Oxon – a knight and wife, *c.* 1480, with saints and the Trinity. Part of a carved altar tomb, now in the churchyard. All the rivets and plugs are lost

Sir Robert Corbet, 1403 (engraved *c.* 1385), Marcham, Berkshire – a tracing from a rubbing by Hinton of a typical Style 'B' knight, stolen in 1837. Photograph by Mark Blackburn; reproduced by courtesy of the Bodleian Library

Plate 2 Two indents in very bad condition: A priest in cope in the head of a cross, *c.* 1380, St Mary the Virgin, Oxford, looking across the top of the slab, with a half-metre scale lying along the indent of the figure.

Crozier and inscription for Abbot John (?) de Bibury, *c.* 1320, Horspath, Oxon (see also Figs 1 and 2)

indents for normal brasses, and a further twenty Flemish incised slabs that have had inlays of brass or composition, not to mention five incised slabs without inlays. Many of the indents for brasses are in Tournai stone, indicating the busy trade of Boston with the Flemish ports, which made imported brasses as available as English ones. Here presumably the silting up of the port and consequent decline in the economy of Boston preserved the slabs, since the impoverished town could not afford to replace them.

Looking at figures on a county basis, it may be worth comparing the number of indents not with the total of surviving brasses but with the total of pre-Reformation brasses only, since the vast majority of known indents are pre-Reformation. Bedfordshire in the 1880s had 109 indents as opposed to 192 brasses, of which 101 were pre-Reformation; the number of pre-Reformation brasses and indents is therefore almost equal. Bedfordshire has long been a Protestant and even Puritan county, and one might have expected a higher rate of loss, as in Huntingdonshire, which is about the same size and was equally Puritan, where only nine medieval brasses survive to forty-eight indents. Here one has to consider the religious element, for these counties were centres of Puritanism and there may really have been some genuine religious iconoclasts as opposed to the opportunists who elsewhere used religion as an excuse for theft. Huntingdonshire is a poorer county than Bedfordshire, however, and there was probably less money available in the nineteenth century for church restoration and the consequent destruction of indents.

Connor lists 238 brasses in Somerset, though only thirty-seven of these are pre-Reformation, as opposed to forty-eight listed indents. Again the proportions are roughly equal, though here in a rural county out of the way of wars and little affected by fanaticism. In West Sussex, however, there are only fifty-two pre-Reformation brasses compared with eighty-seven indents in an equally rural and out of the way county. East Sussex, with virtually no factors to distinguish it from

West Sussex, has fifty-four pre-Reformation brasses and only about forty indents, a very different proportion. Cornwall, about as remote as one can get and tending to be recusant and royalist, has thirty-one pre-Reformation brasses and only about six indents, so that it would appear the county has retained virtually its entire complement of medieval brasses.

These figures do not seem to prove very much. The only conclusion we can draw (and it is a conclusion worth knowing) is that the number of indents surviving in a given church or area is not related to the number of surviving brasses, nor is there any consistent criterion by which such a relation could be established. The factors governing the survival of indents are to a large extent arbitrary—whether or not the church has been repaved, and to what extent the parish could afford or was prepared to pay for new flooring rather than re-using the old indents.

The total number of indents surviving in the country is probably not very different from the number of surviving medieval brasses - probably some two or three thousand. As will be seen in Chapter 5, the majority of lost brasses date from before the Reformation, as one would expect, and indents seem to reflect this. There are very few post-Reformation indents.

THE CATALOGUING OF INDENTS

A surprisingly small proportion of the total number of indents has ever been properly recorded, despite desultory attempts and odd notes by antiquarians ever since the seventeenth century. As a result many indents that could easily have been recorded a century ago have been lost for good. Many of the early antiquaries included a number of drawings of indents in their collections, and Hinton even rubbed some, but they never attempted to make a complete collection for any one area. Not until the end of the nineteenth century was any attempt made to catalogue indents systematically. In the early issues of the *Transactions* of the Cambridge University Association of Brass Collectors (later the Monumental Brass Society) catalogues were made of all the brasses and indents in Bedfordshire, Cambridgeshire (unfinished) and Huntingdonshire. Meanwhile the Oxford University Brass Rubbing Society produced catalogues of brasses and indents in virtually all the churches of Oxford and several in the surrounding counties. These catalogues merely described the indents and sometimes gave their measurements, but did not illustrate them.

Other works dealing systematically with the brasses of a whole county, such as Davis's *Gloucestershire,* Mrs Davidson-Houston's *Sussex,* Morley's *Berkshire* or Griffin and Stephenson's *Kent,* either do not mention indents or include only a few of the finest and most obvious. Connor in his articles on Somerset brasses describes all the indents but illustrates only a few, and the same applies to Mill Stephenson's county series. The Royal Commission on Historical Monuments includes a list of all indents, though without illustrations, but so far it covers only a small part of the country.

Credit for the first attempt to illustrate every indent in a county goes to A. C. Sadler, whose *The Lost Monumental Brasses of West Sussex* and *East Sussex* (1969-70) illustrates all the indents except simple inscriptions and those too worn to be legible, and for the first time records the complete indents of a county. Unfortunately his illustrations are prepared from rubbings, and the worn condition of most of the slabs has led to many inaccuracies. To avoid this, the Oxford University Archaeological Society used measured drawings of the indents themselves for the recent survey of Oxford.[6] The publication of the Sussex and Oxford surveys has illustrated about 180 indents, which is probably as many as had ever been illustrated before from all over Britain. Only two of the Oxford indents had ever been reproduced before, and only about ten from the whole of Sussex. Of other counties, Essex has been best served, some thirty indents having been reproduced by Miller Christy and W. Porteous in a widely scattered series of articles.[7]

Accounts of brasses in individual churches or cathedrals in journals usually include illustrations of some of the best indents: nine from St Alban's were illustrated by Page;[8] and four from Canterbury, two from Rochester and one from Salt-wood by Ralph Griffin.[9] References to others are given under each church in Mill Stephenson's list, but the number is woefully small. Of all the indents in Lincoln, only one has been reproduced. Without illustrations, descriptions of indents, particularly the more unusual or puzzling ones, are of very little use. In any case they continue to be worn away or destroyed, so that an illustration which could have been prepared with ease 50 or 100 years ago can no longer be made.

The author's own work on Sussex and Oxford, moreover, has shown that accurate lists are very rare. Of ninety-three indents or fragments of indents in West Sussex, only sixty-six were included in Sadler's monograph; most of the additional ones were in churchyards or very worn, but a few were important. In Oxford the survey found several indents which the Victorian catalogues had missed, and no less than twenty-one which the Royal Commission had missed. Some indeed were covered until recently, like the one formerly under the organ at Merton College, and nine in All Saints' that were under a carpet (though elsewhere the Royal Commission looked under carpets). On the other hand the Royal Commission listed one and the Brass Rubbing Society two that have since been destroyed, though none of these had been drawn or rubbed.

Indents are not always obvious and it often takes quite a lot of looking from different angles before one will reveal itself. No large slab of the right stone should ever be passed over without a thorough examination, especially out of doors, where the lead plugs, which may be the only remaining evidence, usually weather to exactly the same colour as the stone. A thorough catalogue of indents will be to a certain extent a specialist task.

Indents are still very much neglected by antiquaries or church authorities, and it is often surprising how unobservant people can be. Most incumbents by now have a fairly clear idea of how many and what sort of brasses they possess (not to mention how large a fee they can charge for rubbing them!), but very few have ever realised that the indents may often be of much greater archaeological value and importance. Very few church guides mention indents, even when they commemorate known individuals of importance in the parish. Obviously an incumbent is primarily a minister and cannot be expected to be an archaeologist, but it is slightly alarming to know that archaeological treasures are in the care of non-experts. Nor are such treasures subject to any sort of legal control or protection, and the churches are quite within their rights to remove indents or slabs without planning permission, and frequently do so. Indents are always liable to be removed without warning, especially if they are worn and only visible to an expert eye. Of course, a church is not a museum, and worn stones that convey nothing to any but a very few cannot really be expected to stand in the way of essential repairs or the levelling of an uneven floor; but it is reasonable to ask that such slabs should be recorded properly before they go. Then, since such a slab is usually quite anonymous, there is no disrespect to the dead in removing it. Obviously indents in good condition, especially when they show outlines for fine or unusual brasses, ought to be preserved whenever possible, but again, if the worst comes to the worst, an adequate record is sufficient. Indeed, it does not seem worth while normally recommending the removal of indents from redundant churches except in very special circumstances.

RECORDING TECHNIQUES

Leaving out the obviously ideal but impractical possibility of casts, there are four practical ways of recording indents—rubbing, dabbing, photography and drawing have been used.

All have their particular advantages and disadvantages.

Rubbing Indents
Rubbing is perhaps the most obvious answer, as an extension of simple brass-rubbing. No brass-rubbing is worth anything unless it includes the indents of lost parts, and these are usually rubbed simply by outlining the edges of the indents. When rubbing an indent for a totally lost brass, it is usual to rub the slab and leave the indents white, and preferably to rub the whole surface of the slab to avoid confusion. Where the edges of the indents are still sharp and clear, it is quite easy to run the heelball along them and produce a definite outline. The surface of the stone should not be rubbed too hard, but evenly, to produce a grey textured rubbing that approximates to the colour and texture of the slab. Wherever possible, the whole slab should be rubbed, as far as the edge all round.

Few people, when rubbing indents, attempt to do anything about the rivets or other relics of the fixing of the brass, yet these are important and ought to be included in the rubbing. Empty plug-holes and lead plugs are usually fairly easy to indicate by outlining the edge of the hole or rubbing the surface of the lead. Worn rivets can be rubbed likewise, but upstanding rivets are difficult and cannot be more than indicated on the paper. The channels for water to run down and cool the lead plugs are also significant and should be included, as should the deepenings on early indents to hold the batons by which the plates were fastened together. Nearly all these features at the bottom of indents cannot be rubbed without tearing the paper, so the rubber must be prepared for this to happen, and patch up the rubbing afterwards (see Plate 3a).

Difficulty arises when, as in the majority of cases, the indent is worn or flaked. Rubbings showing only the unflaked surface are common, but these can lead to serious misinterpretation as outlines become blurred or misshapen. Whole extra figures have been invented on published indents drawn from rubbings of the level surfaces only, when the rubber has not made certain whether or not parts, or all of the now sunken areas were originally cut away. Looking at the slab, it is usually easy to see which parts have been deliberately cut away to make an indent and which have flaked accidentally. The only way to rub such slabs is to fasten the paper securely at one end only and unroll it slowly as the rubbing is made, constantly rolling back to check where the outline really is, and following it with a sharp-pointed piece of heelball. By this method a convincing rubbing can be made of a virtually smooth slab, but it calls for some skill in interpretation and accuracy of observation during the rubbing (see Plate 3b). Where an indent has not even approximate edges but simply appears as a gentle dip in the surface of the stone, it is virtually impossible to produce a rubbing, though the rivets and other accessories may still be recorded.

The great advantage of a rubbing is that it is full size, accurate and objective. The whole slab is reproduced on the original scale, the relation of the parts to each other is exact, and one can be certain that all the rivets and plugs are shown in their precise positions. This is especially valuable when the rubbing is taken to a museum or elsewhere to compare with a loose brass that is suspected of belonging to that indent; outlines of figures are often alike, but the exact pattern of rivets can be matched to the holes in the brass exactly and an identification made with certainty. Sizes and shapes of various parts can also easily be compared with similar parts of other indents or surviving brasses in work on stylistic analysis.

The size of a rubbing, however, can also rank as a disadvantage. Rubbings of large indents are very cumbersome, requiring a lot of storage space and even more for examination. An attempt, for instance, to compare a rubbing of Bishop Beaumont's indent in Durham, which is 4.5 by 2.7m, with that of Bishop de Haselshaw at Wells, 4.5 by 1.9m (both considerably larger than any surviving brass in the world), would require a clear floor space 4½m square simply to lay them out, let alone walk round them and look at them. A further disadvantage of rubbing is that it is dependent on the skill and accuracy of the rubber. Though rubbings of brasses and well-defined indents are completely objective, and one can be sure that any competent rubbing is accurate, once we get to worn or flaking indents the rubber virtually has to draw the outlines for himself as described above, which is where the skill comes in.

Furthermore, whereas brass-rubbing does little or no harm to the metal, there is a genuine doubt whether rubbing is detrimental to the surface of slabs. Obviously not enough people will ever want to rub indents for this to become a real threat, but many churches may refuse permission for rubbings to be made on these grounds, besides the more obvious objection to encumbering the church.

Dabbing Indents

Many authorities in the past have recommended dabbing as an alternative to rubbing for indents. A dabbing is made on tissue paper with blackened leather, either mounted on a pad or wrapped round the finger. The leather is prepared by 'charging' it on a board coated with a paste of powdered graphite in olive oil, and it is rubbed gently on the tissue in the same manner as a heelball rubbing. The advantage of this technique is that it allows rubbings to be made with much finer detail than is possible with thicker paper, and it is also much less strenuous and quicker than a heelball rubbing. For indents a dabbing was favoured as giving a closer approximation to the texture of the stone, and being able to pick up worn edges where the heelball could not. Many of the great Cambridge collection of rubbings include a dabbing of the indent attached to a rubbing of the surviving brass.

On the other hand the disadvantages of dabbing probably outweigh its advantages. It is now possible to get paper as thin as tissue paper but strong enough to stand up to ordinary rubbing, and this has the great advantage that it does not crinkle as easily as tissue. Storage of large sheets of tissue is very much more difficult than storage of ordinary paper, and dabbings are much more fragile than rubbings. Moreover a soft rounded dabber cannot make precise lines like a stick of heelball, and would be inadequate on a worn indent where outlines need to be defined clearly. The process itself is also much more difficult, as it needs care to get an unstreaked coverage, it is messy and it involves more equipment.

Photographing Indents

Direct photography of indents is much easier than photographing brasses, since indents do not reflect light so much and have a better contrast. However, there remains the problem of foreshortening, and unless the camera can be held directly over the centre of the slab at a height sufficient to include the whole composition, a certain amount of distortion is inevitable. A wide-angle lens is no solution, as the edges of the photograph would still be distorted. Details, of course, can easily be photographed vertically, but an indent of any size would require an exceptionally large tripod to give a vertical view. Mural slabs and indents are much easier, as one can stand back from them.[10]

When a slab is worn, however, it is usually essential to take the photograph at an angle anyway, as slight depressions and faint indents often show up only when viewed obliquely. An oblique photograph, especially with oblique lighting to heighten the shadows, will often show far more detail on a very worn slab than a rubbing or dabbing can possibly do (see Plate 2b). The slab usually shows up to its best advantage at one particular angle, and frequently at a certain time of day. Slabs in churchyards have sometimes been observed to reveal traces of indents only in wet weather.[11] A photograph has the advantage that it can capture the moment when the indent is at its best, and it is also completely objective. Moreover, if the indent is in a carved or moulded frame or is part of a large monument with carved stonework, a photograph alone will show this, and record the indent in the setting to which it belongs. Where a brass only formed part of an elaborate monument, it conveys a false impression to record only the indents and not the rest of the composition.

Photographs have, of course, the inestimable advantage that they are far easier to store, to consult and compare than rubbings or dabbings could ever be. A collection of several thousand photographs can easily be contained in a single cabinet, and selections can be made for interpretation or comparison. Slides are virtually indispensible for lecturing, as large rubbings of indents cannot conveniently be displayed or held up in any numbers. The principal disadvantages of photography would seem to be the foreshortening mentioned above, and the necessity of increasing the angle so much when a worn indent is involved that it is impossible to reconstruct the correct proportions. Photography also suffers from the poor light in many churches, especially when indents are found, as they often are, in particularly dark and obscure corners. Finally, of course, photography is expensive.

Drawing Indents

The fourth method, of measured scale drawings, seems at first to be the least reliable and most difficult, but it manages to avoid the most serious drawbacks of the other methods without losing too much in accuracy. Archaeologists have never relied on photographs alone, but have always insisted on drawing and planning everything by hand. Drawings can be to a large extent interpretations made in the field, and are much easier to read and understand than photographs. In a drawing the most important points can be highlighted, and by the use of conventions a more intelligible picture can be presented than in any other way.

Drawings of indents were made by several antiquaries of the late eighteenth and early nineteenth centuries, notably Thomas Fisher, some of whose drawings of Kentish indents were reproduced by Ralph Griffin.[12] His drawings show the outline clearly, mark the rivets and water channels, and are ideal for interpretation or comparison. Since then, however, the few indents that have been reproduced have been reduced from rubbings or dabbings, so that again it was the Oxford survey that was the first in modern times to experiment on a large scale with drawings. At a conference of the Monumental Brass Society in 1972 several members worked on surveying indents in Wells Cathedral by different methods, and a few drawings were made by taking measurements of all the component parts of each indent and transferring them to squared paper. This method was taken up in Oxford and developed, using some of the techniques of field archaeology. The taking of measurements was simplified by the use of a 1m-square wire grid, wired at 10cm intervals, which was placed over the indent, whose outlines were copied directly on to squared paper. To ensure the grid remained in position, and as a guide to aligning the next square, little chalk marks were made on the slabs, from which they could easily be cleaned afterwards. An alternative method used on simpler indents was to stretch a tape along the slab, and measure points and offsets along it. By either method it was found that indents could be copied quickly and accurately, with less mess and bother than rubbing and more cheaply than photography.

A problem that neither rubbings nor photographs could solve was how to distinguish indents that were strongly defined from those that were faint or largely conjectural. A rubbing of a worn slab shows a well-defined outline, even though the outline on the slab might be faint. (Plate 3b is a case in point, where the outlines look clear though they are barely visible in reality.) This problem was easily avoided on drawings by giving a solid line to existing outlines and a broken line to those that were conjectural. The shape of the whole indent is thus immediately clear to the observer; it is also clear where the outlines are the recorder's interpretation, and it is open to the student to make his own interpretations at these points (Figs 1 and 2).

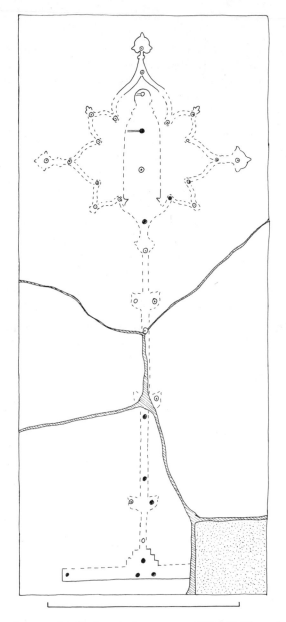

1   A priest in cope in the head of a cross, c1380, St Mary the Virgin,
Oxford - a drawing of an indent in very bad condition. Compare the direct
photograph, Plate 2a

In the Oxford method conventionally surviving rivets were marked as black dots within circles, lead plugs as shaded circles, empty plug-holes as open circles, cement patching as shading and stone insertions as stippling. Water channels and other features were marked on, as were cracks in the stone if this did not obscure the essential features. Later appropriations were always marked. In a drawing these cracks and appropriations can be seen to be secondary, whereas in a rubbing they would be the most prominent features; in a photograph discolourations in the stone or shadows often predominate.

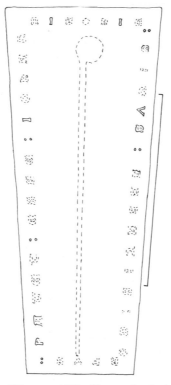

2   Abbot John (?) de Bibury, c1320, Horspath, Oxfordshire - a drawing of an indent in very bad condition. Compare with photograph, Plate 2b. A crozier brass with inscription in separate letters

The techniques for drawing from indents can also be applied for reducing drawings from rubbings if the original indents are inaccessible. The drawings once made are easily copied, either by transferring them on to further sheets of squared paper, or tracing them on to clean sheets to produce a clear drawing of the slab for publication. A 1m scale is inserted to allow for variations in the scale of reduction. The originals are nearly all drawn at 1:10, though a few may be done at 1:20.

There can be no doubt that drawings are easier to interpret than photographs or rubbings, and they have the photograph's advantage of being small and easy to handle. For reproduction they are very much easier and far cheaper, as they can be printed as line drawings rather than half-tones. They overcome the difficulties of recording worn indents as no other method can, and they are also cheaper and quicker. A great advantage of this is that the simpler indents of plain inscriptions or effaced examples with only two or three rivets preserved can be copied so quickly that there is no excuse for neglecting them. Since rubbings and photography take longer and are more complicated, there is always a temptation to save time and trouble by forgetting such indents.

The disadvantages of drawings are that they rely very much on the accuracy of the recorder, and on his ability to interpret faint shapes and outlines, as well as demanding a certain amount of skill in drawing and an ability to abstract shapes and reproduce them accurately—the same skills that are needed in archaeological planning. The ideal would be to have rubbings, photographs and scale drawings of all indents, and certainly all indents in good condition should be recorded on rubbings and photographs wherever possible, though normally any interpretive work can best be done on the drawings alone.

Records and Their Dissemination
Besides copying it in some way, it is important to record other

facts about the indent before leaving the church. If it is not clear from the reproduction, the size of the slab should be noted, as should its position in the church, churchyard or elsewhere, and, if possible, the type of stone from which it is made. It is also useful to note the date on which the record was made for future reference. Besides this it is worth looking in the church guide to see if there is any tradition of whom the slab commemorates.

The mass of material that would be accumulated in making a set of rubbings, photographs and drawings of all indents could only be housed in a major museum, and access would almost certainly have to be limited. It is therefore worth publishing illustrations of indents if possible, since all archaeological work that is not published is to a great extent wasted. Such publication is usually best done in a local or national learned journal, though Mr Sadler has shown that it is possible to produce a privately printed monograph on lost brasses.

In the published version of the Oxford survey every indent was reproduced except for simple indents of inscriptions and a few that were no more than a meaningless scatter of rivets (though drawings of these were deposited in the Archaeological Society's archives). Notes were included on their subject matter, size and location of the slab, and type of stone if differing from the normal Purbeck marble. When the slab had been numbered by the Royal Commission, its reference was given. At Oxford this was done in conjunction with a summary of the documentary evidence for lost brasses, and the whole was written up in chronological order for each church in turn. A simple record of indents without the documentary report would still be of great value and would be much easier to compile. It could be arranged either chronologically or, following the Royal Commission and others, in topographical order within each church. In the case of a large church or cathedral with many indents it is often impossible to allot dates accurately enough to make a chronological sequence, and a sequence in order of location makes it easier to find and identify the slabs in the future.

It would be very useful if anyone contemplating a work on the brasses of any particular county or area would include all indents and illustrate as many as possible so that the work may be complete. The most recent county series-Connor's *Somerset* and Dr Cameron's *Middlesex*-do indeed include notes on all indents, but illustrate only a few. Since rubbings exist of every brass in Britain, so that no brass can now be lost without a record remaining, it seems less important to illustrate brasses thoroughly than to illustrate indents of which no adequate record yet exists. It is to be hoped that in future this work will be carried out as an integral part of any further work on surviving brasses.

THE INTERPRETATION OF INDENTS

The first steps towards the interpretation of an indent can only be done in the church itself by noting those technical details of the slab that cannot be recorded by rubbing, photography or drawing. Of these the most important is the type of stone, as this gives a very important clue to the probable origin of the brass.

The vast majority of brasses laid in England were set in Purbeck marble, a shelly fossiliferous limestone from Dorset. When cut and polished, the fossil shells show in section, giving a mottled effect. The colour is usually some shade of grey, occasionally with a green or red tinge. Most of the London workshops used Purbeck for their brasses, and it is found all over the country. A very similar stone is Petworth marble, which in other beds is known as Wealden or Bethersden marble. This tends to contain larger shells, and is consequently more liable to crumble and perish. Although there is no evidence for a local Sussex workshop, Sussex brasses of London style are often set in it, and it would appear that the brasses were sometimes sent out from London to be set in

Plate 3 Rubbings of indents: An indent in good condition – Ralph Shurley and wife, 1510, with Trinity, two sons and three daughters, Wiston, Sussex. Note that there are no water channels on this slab, and most of the rivets are lost

An indent in poor condition – a man in armour and two wives, *c.* 1490, with surviving children, Thenford, Northamptonshire. The rivets and water channels survive, but the outlines are worn smooth

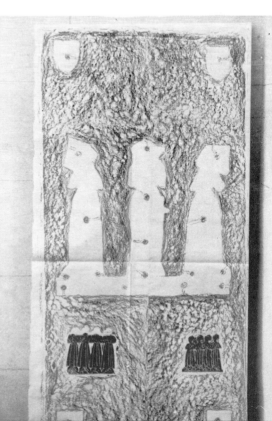

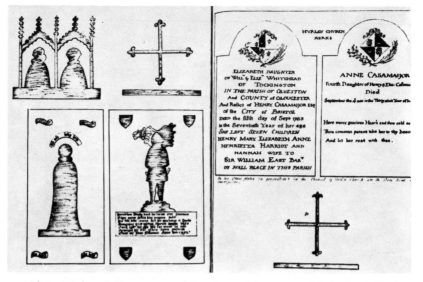

Plate 4 (above) Two pages of drawings of brasses and indents at Hurley, Berkshire; *(below)* Thomas Bartlet, 1675, St Ebbe's, Oxford – a drawing of a late and unusual type of rectangular plate. Two items from the Hinton Collection, reproduced by courtesy of the Bodleian Library.

their slabs locally. The same argument applies to some West Country indents in dark blue lias stone, which is very hard and brittle. London brasses are found in this local stone, though it was used by a West Country workshop and its use may point to the brass having been made locally also.

Among other local stones is Oxford stone, a pale yellow freestone that may point out the products of the Oxford workshop, though again we find London brasses set in it. Allerton marble is used in Yorkshire, and other stones are occasionally found. A curious indent at King's Sutton, Northamptonshire, which shows very crude figures, is set in a very local Jurassic limestone full of fossil belemnites, both of which characteristics seem to imply that we have here the only evidence for a small workshop in that area. In fact, as far the majority of slabs are in Purbeck marble, the use of another stone may often, though by no means always, point to the brass having been made locally.

The use of the very dark blue or black Tournai stone for slabs certainly indicates that the brasses have been imported from the Ghent, Tournai and Bruges area. Despite the vast size of most of these brasses, they were always imported complete with their slabs (which frequently had to be made up in sections), and Tournai stone is found all over Europe from Gdańsk to Madeira. Every one of the twenty-seven known Scots indents is in Tournai stone, and many have been found in England. Even when the indent is completely effaced or even laid upside down, the stone would give it away as Flemish. The majority are found along the east coast, but they also penetrated inland. In the West Country care should be taken not to confuse Tournai stone with the local blue lias.

The method of fixing the brass will also offer clues to its date and provenance. The earliest brasses were simply glued down with a layer of pitch. Large figures and canopies that were made up of more than one sheet of brass were joined at the back by a strip of metal, for which a deepening had to be cut in the indent and which served as an anchor for the brass.

These deepenings in bands across the figure are an invariable sign of a brass dating from before the Black Death.

Rivets were introduced about 1330, and the use of backing strips died out soon afterwards. Only a very few indents show traces of both together, such as that of Adam de Brome, 1332, at St Mary's, Oxford. Early rivets are closely spaced, but later ones are larger and placed further apart. The pattern of rivets often reveals how many plates were used to make up the brass. Large Flemish quadrangular brasses were made up of several plates each, and their outlines can be detected from the lines of rivets in the slab.

The occasional use of wooden plugs instead of lead generally indicates mural brasses, though it is not yet quite clear why this method was used. An indent in Christ Church, Oxford, now on the floor, has wooden plugs which indicate that it has been removed from the wall, a fact corroborated by traces of moulding round the edges of the slab. Any other method of fixing indicated in the indent is almost certainly a sign that the brass had been refixed at some time, and may indicate that it is not the original slab. A slab that does not show indents for the whole composition is obviously not the original, though further search may reveal the latter elsewhere in the church. At St Lawrence, Reading, a surviving mural brass apparently shows a man beside a very much smaller figure of his wife, and on the floor nearby is an indent for the same arrangement. Out in the graveyard, however, lies the real indent, showing that the surviving plates are only part of a large composition, and that the small female figure is in fact one of three daughters, not the wife, who was of the same size as her husband.

Measuring the depth of the indents may occasionally provide a clue to the date of the brass, since very thick plates were used before about 1400 and after about 1620, and thinner plates between. However, the depth of indents, besides being difficult to measure accurately, is affected by the amount of wear on the surface, and is unreliable as evidence. Measuring the depth of plug-holes does not seem to lead to anything, though further research may find significant differences in the technique of fixing.

The bulk of indent interpretation must, of course, be done from the outlines alone, and the art lies very much in being able to recognise the outlines of brasses without their internal lines. Certain types are quite standard and obvious. Bishops and abbots are easily distinguishable by the mitre and crozier, and archbishops by having a cross instead of a crozier. Most military figures are marked by the pointed helmet, the outline of the sword, and, above all, by the gap between the legs that can only appear on armoured figures. Ladies invariably have long skirts trailing on the ground, while the gowns of male civilians and priests usually stop short of the ground. Dates can usually be refined to about 10 years either way, based on regular typologies such as armour or female headdress. Priests are more difficult to date, as the style of vestments does not change. Mass vestments have a distinctive outline because of the sleeveless chasuble, and processional vestments show up clearly, with a straight falling cope and bulge round the neck for the almuce; but the only change that occurs is their tendency to become shorter and more squat with the passing of the years. The hair style may be more helpful, as it was long and flowing in the fourteenth century, close-cropped in the fifteenth and lank and straight in the sixteenth. Occasionally the tonsure shows in indents, which helps to distinguish priests from those civilians who wore similar hair styles.

The only way to recognise outlines is to study rubbings or illustrations of all the standard types of brass at different periods and compare the outlines. It may be helpful to trace the outlines off an illustrated list such as the Victoria and Albert Museum's catalogue. Certain types can give a very distinctive outline that is impossible to describe verbally. Often something shown in the stance of the figure, such as the slight sway of the hips in the mid-thirteenth century, gives it away. Occasionally, however, there are real difficulties. Academics are very difficult to sort out from coped priests and even from some civilians, and the lack of a consistent typology of gowns makes it almost impossible to identify them with any accuracy. A distinctive feature is the academic cap, which fits tightly to the head, leaving a round impression; occasionally a lock of hair escapes on each side of it. The same outline, however, may be given by the coif worn by serjeants-at-law and judges. Technically the academic cap should have a little point, but this usually does not show on indents. An example in Oxford Cathedral closely resembles a surviving academic in New College, but he is equipped with a wife and is clearly a lawyer, not an academic. Other difficult outlines are produced by odd forms of costume that distort the figure, such as the wide upstanding hood worn by women in the early seventeenth century, which is always liable to be confused with a cushion under the head.

Indents can often be dated and identified fairly closely by small details, so even very fragmentary indents can be interpreted. The outline of the head alone is the most distinctive part, but close datings can be made by sword hilts, lions or other footrests, or even by the fall of the garments.

Canopies, shields and even inscriptions can be as distinctive as figures. On a very worn indent it may be difficult to sort out the pinnacles of a complicated canopy, but this sort of feature is usually easy to reconstruct. Canopy types vary according to date, the later ones usually becoming heavier and clumsier than the earlier. Shields are occasionally topped by helmets and crests, which on early brasses are cut out so that the outlines are often clear enough to decipher the crest and so identify the family commemorated. On later examples, however, the mantling or cloth hanging from the helmet tends to obscure the outlines, and it became normal eventually to engrave coats of arms on rectangular plates. Inscription plates are not very often distinctive in outline, though marginal inscriptions can show peculiarities that may help to date them; but it is worth recording indents of inscriptions, since there is always the chance of identifying them from a surviving rubbing. The indent of William Scot (Fig 3) in St Mary's, Oxford, was finally identified by comparing the pattern of rivets in the indent for the foot inscription with the holes shown on the print in the Gough collection.[13]

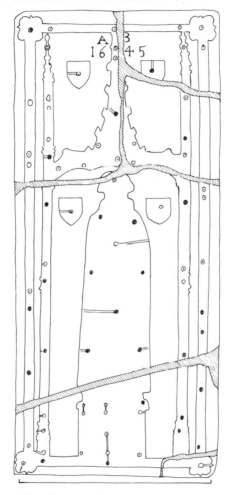

3   William Scot, priest in cope, 1441, St Mary the Virgin, Oxford - an indent in good condition but cracked and patched with cement, and appropriated by initials in 1645

Many brasses never included figures, the central motif being a cross, crozier, chalice, heart or other device. Normally it is fairly easy to recognise these, though the variety in types and forms is almost infinite. Many devices found outlined on indents have no surviving parallel. Some have remained unidentifiable, such as the devices on the Trotton and Saltwood slabs (Fig 28), but most can be deciphered. Dating them, however, is very difficult, as they occur spasmodically throughout the medieval period.

There are also a great variety of religious devices and figures, some of which are very difficult to recognise. Figures of saints in canopies can hardly ever be identified from indents alone, though sets of twelve are likely to be the Apostles. Angels are usually found on canopies or flanking the head of the figure, and are easily distinguishable by their wings. The Holy Trinity is the most popular group; usually the design has a distinctive outline, though occasionally it is obscured by being placed in a frame of some sort. The Virgin and Child may appear in a similar frame, or in an oval frame or mandorla, but normally the figures are cut out so as to be recognisable. Annunciations are common, and can be distinguished as two kneeling figures (one winged), with scrolls and often a lily pot, and God the Father on a cloud above (see the one on the lost brass at St Margaret's, Westminster, Fig 4).

Confusing indents may give rise to some curious misinterpretations. At Chalgrove, Oxfordshire, the Oxford University Brass Rubbing Society refixed a small inscription upside down above the indent of a shield, and then, looking at the indent upside down, referred to it as 'something like a beehive'.[14] Other shapes liable to mislead are arrangements of scrolls, banners construed as meat cleavers, or rectangular plates holding Trinities or coats of arms seen as secondary inscriptions.

A category that can be very difficult to interpret without experience is the Flemish incised slab with indents for inlays of brass or composition. Frequently the incised lines are worn away, and all that is visible is the indentation for highlighting parts of the design. Usually these are the hands and face, but other parts such as belts, patches of embroidery on clothes, shoes, sword pommels, figures of saints and angels, shields, evangelistic symbols or inscriptions could also be inlaid. All Hallows, Barking, London, possesses the remains of such a memorial, where the inscription, head and hands and the wings of two angels survive in brass in a totally effaced incised slab. The head and hands are also totally effaced, and for a long time were loose. Since the tips of the fingers joined on to the neck, making a single piece of brass, the whole plate rather resembles a mallet, and it is as such that it is usually described. Normally a gap is left between the neckline and the fingertips, so this sort of confusion is not likely to occur often. Where other parts are inlaid, a reconstruction can only be made if one remembers that vital parts were incised in the stone, and the brass plates were never intended to stand on their own. It should also be remembered that these inlays were not always brass, but were often of composition or coloured marble; and the indents for such inlays would be deeper than those for brass, and would not show any trace of riveting.

Notes for this chapter appear on page 186

4

DOCUMENTARY SOURCES

The inscription und' it which was engraven on a brass plate,
having been time out of mind theeved away, I was forced to
consult my obscure oracle who in his notes written an. 1574, I
find y^t ye effect of it ran thus . . . (Anthony Wood)

Although our most objective sources for information on lost
brasses are indents, by far the bulk of our material must come
from documentary sources. Information on thousands of
brasses now lost without trace can be extracted from a be-
wilderingly wide variety of chance references, antiquarian
collections, notes, drawings and rubbings. Records, once they
have appeared in print, may be virtually guaranteed to outlast
the brasses they refer to.

The documentary sources span a period as wide as the
brasses themselves, beginning in the fourteenth century. By
far the fullest and most useful are, of course, the collections of
seventeenth-century and later antiquarians, but much valuable material is known to us only from scanty and passing
notes in earlier sources.

INCIDENTAL SOURCES

Antiquarianism was not a concern of the Middle Ages, and
the documents we have from the crucial centuries before the
dissolution of the monasteries are tantalisingly brief. Never-

theless useful information may be gathered from wills, bills of sale, churchwardens' accounts, obit books and fabric rolls.

Among medieval wills the most famous is that of Sir John Foxle, whose brass in fact survives at Bray, Berkshire. His will describes the brass in great detail, and it is in a way unfortunate that it does not describe a lost brass! Usually, however, medieval wills are brief in their specifications for a brass.

The will of Robert Bagworth of Southampton, 19 May 1477, who was to be buried in Hackney, Middlesex, says 'I wyll that myn executours bye and do ley a stone of marbell upon my grave of the price of xxvjs viijd. w^t an Image knelyng proporcioned aftir the leigh and brede of the said stone w^t day and yere of my decesse and w^t a Rolle in myn handes of this reson, Jhū mercy Lady helpc.'[1] And John Norbury, priest, who was to be buried in Stoke d'Abernon, Surrey, wills on 8 March 1540-1 'that my executours do bye a stone and a picture w^t my name, to ly upon me after I am departed, as sone as they cane convenanly.'[2]

The most detailed of all is that of Thomas Salter, priest of London, whose will of 31 August 1558 provided for his burial in the parish church of St Magnus—with a brass of a priest in Mass vestments, holding a chalice and Host, his eyes shown closed 'as all dead mens eyes ought so to be', and a prayer scroll, a foot inscription with prayers for his soul, and the arms of the Salters Company to which he had once belonged. Moreover he specifies that it is to be engraved by 'a cunynge marbler that dwellithe in sancte Dunstons parishe in the west agaynst the sowth syde of the church'.[3] It is unlikely that these instructions were ever carried out, since the accession of Queen Elizabeth in 1558 put a stop to vestments and prayers for the soul.

Besides wills there are a few surviving contracts for brasses now lost, and a very detailed one, for a brass at Basingstoke ordered from Flanders, is quoted in *Brasses and Brass Rubbing in England*.[4] The ledger of Andrew Halyburton, a

Scots agent in Flanders, mentions several Flemish tombs and brasses imported into Scotland, one of which seems to have been re-used for the brass of the Regent Murray in Edinburgh. The accounts for the making of this brass include an item 'to David Rowane for the same platt of bras . . . vi li.' Presumably Rowane was a speculator in monastic spoil that was fittingly used for the brass of a spoiler of monasteries.[5]

There are a great many passing references to brasses in the documents illustrating their destruction, notably the bills of sale of monastic plunder, churchwardens' accounts, and Dowsing's diary, as already described. Most of these simply tell us the number and weight of brasses, but Dowsing does give us the names of a few brasses, and very helpfully identifies the brass in Trinity Hall from which he removed the inscription as 'Mr Culiard, a Fellow'.[6]

In addition to these we have a few contemporary descriptions of monastic churches, with lists of burials compiled primarily as necrologies—lists of past benefactors to be commemorated each year at Prime on their anniversaries. Because of this they often give the day and month of death, but not the year. A list of 581 burials in the London Greyfriars survives in a manuscript in the British Museum called the *Registrum fratrum minorum Londonie* of 1526. Stow tells us that seven score of these had brasses. The entries are brief notes, many of which have the look of being extracts from funerary inscriptions. Ironically the only tombstone to survive from the church is not included in the list.

A manuscript quoted by Gough describes St Alban's Abbey in 1429, mentioning several brasses on abbots' tombs.[7] But only one and a half survive, and the descriptions are too brief to be of much help. We know that Abbots de la Mare and Mentmore had magnificent Flemish brasses, but the author describes them simply as 'marble stones with their epitaphs inserted'.

A much more detailed account was given by a former monk of Durham, who describes nineteen brasses, including eight of bishops and nine of priors, of which only eleven indents survive. The descriptions range from brief notes to the full and elaborate description of the immense brass of Bishop Beaumont, 1333. The indent for this survives (part of the brass has recently been restored), and agrees precisely with the description of one of the series of large early English brasses now represented only by half a figure at York.[8]

The best of all medieval descriptions is the famous account of the Hastings brass at Elsing, which fills in the details now missing, including the inscription. As most of the brass survives, however, the account is more useful as an indication of what it looked like in the early fifteenth century, and as a reliable source for naming parts of armour, than as a record of lost brasses.[9]

Later, after the Renaissance, chance references are more selfconsciously antiquarian, and consequently may give a fuller picture than the early accounts, which are often interested only in the name and date. Passing references in architects' reports may often give vital clues for reconstructing what they destroyed. The tale of destruction during the nineteenth century is largely known from such references that may, incidentally, be the only sources for the existence of the brasses in the first place.

ITINERARIES

A class of literature that often contributes a great deal to our knowledge of brasses is the itinerary. These documents, of which a number survive, are the accounts, often in diary form, of journeys throughout England undertaken by educated men. Usually the journeys had military or business purposes but, unlike the vast majority of such travellers, these writers saw and noticed things of interest, and have preserved for us not only records of lost brasses but also fascinating pictures of the state of England at various times.

The earliest of the itineraries, one of the most valuable antiquarian documents from the Middle Ages, is that of William
Worcestre,[10] who travelled between 1477 and 1480. He was
chiefly interested in architecture, but does tell us a little about
tombs and brasses. For instance, he mentions the tombs of
eleven lords and ladies in Sele Priory, Sussex, but no trace of
them survives; and he quotes a ten-line Latin hexameter inscription undoubtedly from a brass for William Elmham,
1403, at Bury St Edmunds Abbey. Nothing remains of it now,
and there does not seem to be any other source for it. Worcestre measured most of the churches he visited by pacing them
out, and in so doing must have walked over hundreds of
brasses, but unfortunately he tells us nothing of them.

The next great itinerarian from the close of the Middle
Ages was John Leland. He travelled very widely as a civil ser-
vant between 1535 and 1543, and his itinerary includes copious notes on many subjects. His records of brasses vary very
much from full descriptions with transcripts of the inscriptions to tantalisingly brief notes such as '*In insula Bor. Wytte
Epus Sarum cum imagine aenea deaurata* (Bishop Wytte of
Salisbury has a gilded brass in the North Aisle.') He records a
number of very important brasses, such as that at Newark,
where 'Constance, doughter to Peter, King of Castelle, and
wife to John of Gaunt, liith afore the high altare in a tumbe of
marble with an image of brasse like a quene on it'.[11] He preserves what must have been the original inscription on the
brass of King Ethelred at Wimborne Minster, died 872,
brass engraved c 1400, though he gives the date as 827, which
may have been that on the original inscription now replaced
by a seventeenth-century restoration. At Glastonbury he describes the tombs of King Arthur and Queen Guenevere, which
he claims were constructed by Abbot Swansey (1189-1218),
but, of course, he was wrong in supposing any brasses to be
Swansey's work; there were recurrent bouts of interest in King
Arthur, particularly after the accession of Henry VII, and the
brasses could have been made then. Gough retails a 'vulgar

tradition' that these two tombs are the altar tombs with indents now in St John's, Glastonbury, though Connor more prosaically ascribes them to a late fifteenth-century merchant and wife.[12]

Leland also tells of destruction of brasses in his time, such as that of Bishop Lacey, 1455, at Exeter, 'whos tumbe Heines Dene of Excester defacid'; and Robert Burnell, Bishop of Wells, who 'lay not many yeres since in a high tumbe with an image of brasse, now undre a plain marble'.[13]

Leland, however, was not an archaeologist, and did not often trouble to describe the tombs he mentions. Usually all he gives us is a list of burials, stating whereabouts in the church they are, but not specifying if they are brass or stone. If they survive, or are known from other sources, his information on the original locations can be helpful, but alone it does not tell us very much.

In the seventeenth century we find two useful itineraries compiled by soldiers. The first is *A Relation of a Short Survey of the Western Counties* made by a Lieutenant of the Military Company in Norwich in 1635, who has been identified as one Lieutenant Hammond.[14] Despite the title, most of Hammond's travelling seems to have taken place in the eastern and southern counties, and his notes are especially useful in giving us a picture of the status quo before the outbreak of war. For instance, as already mentioned, he reveals that much of the damage normally attributed to the Civil War was already done. His notes of surviving brasses are rather scanty. Those on Malden in Essex mention 'many fayre Gravestones there, with pretty Inscriptions in French and Latine, which for want of time I could not take', and those on Salisbury record that 'There is a rich and rare peece all of Brasse in hand to be set up, in the Lady Chappell for the Earle of Pembroke late Lord Chamberlaine'; but elsewhere he only gives vague references to 'faire Marble Gravestones' and the like.

A much more valuable source is the diary of Richard Symonds, an officer in the king's army, who took part in the siege of Oxford, 1643-4. He was evidently bored during the long confinement, and wandered about the city taking notes of the inscriptions on brasses. Unfortunately a section of the resulting Oxford church notes is missing, but the surviving parts are useful for comparison with Wood's postwar survey in showing precisely what damage (and how little) was done during the Civil War.[15]

The bulk of Symonds's work is contained in the main diary, compiled as he followed the king around the country on campaign. He seems to have seized every opportunity to slip into the nearest church and record brasses and stained glass. Sometimes he was evidently pressed for time, but at others he was able to take adequate notes, as at Blandford in Dorset where he describes the brass to Anne Delalynde in great detail, blazoning all the extremely complicated heraldry and giving the inscription in full. Anne Delalynde, afterwards Browne, 1563, was the daughter of Sir William Goring, whose unusual brass at Burton, Sussex, is described and illustrated in *Brasses and Brass Rubbing in England* (p 50, 103). It is fairly clear from Symonds's description that the Blandford brass was very similar, and also showed the woman wearing a tabard of arms. It was engraved at the cost of her brother George Goring in 1564. Symonds provides an equally detailed description of another brass, to Sir John Rogers, in the same church, 'in armour of our modern fashion', and his wife, 1565, and mentions two more. In addition to listing brasses, he includes notes on indents, for instance, at Llandaff Cathedral, 'Six monuments of bishops in all in this church. Whereof is a flat stone inlayed in brasse, the brasse gone', and at Braunstone, Northamptonshire, 'A playne course altar monument which has beene inlayed with brass, four shields, two pictures, all gone, in the chancel'.[16]

After the Civil War the greatest of the itinerarians was the antiquarian parson Dr William Stukeley. In 1734 he published his *Itinerarium Curiosum*, an account of a succession

of travels about the country in which each journey is dignified
with a title in Latin such as *'Domesticum'* or *'Romanum'*. His
principal interests were the Roman and prehistoric periods,
and he in fact invented the legend connecting Stonehenge with
the Druids, but on his travels he also noted medieval antiquities, including brasses. Like most of the itinerarians he is very
arbitrary in what he records, often ignoring large and spectacular brasses and noting only the less significant ones. This
practice is useful to us, however, since he records many monuments beneath the notice of other antiquaries. For instance,
after describing the Roman city of Verulamium he paid a cur-
sory visit to St Alban's Abbey noticing none of the brasses,
but then visited St Peter's Church where (p 111) he 'found this
old inscription on a stone, EDITHE : LE : VINETER : GIST : ICI :
DIEV : DE : SA : ALME : EIT : MERCI (Edith le Vineter lies here,
God have mercy on her soul). The Abbey brasses were well recorded by Weever, as were the large and spectacular brasses
in St Peter's but Stukeley is the only source for this inscription, which is undoubtedly one of the early fourteenth-century
slabs with separate-letter inscriptions in brass. (In fact Stukeley seems to have specialised in recording this sort of slab,
possibly under the belief that they were earlier than in fact
they were. All antiquaries of the period call the lettering
'Saxon letters', and may have thought they were really
Saxon.) In Lincoln Stukeley notes that 'I found this inscription on a stone in the stable-wall of the *Rain-deer* inn. + RAN-
DOLF : DE : BORTON : GYT : ICY : DEVS : DE : SA : ALME : EYT :
MERCY : AMEN'. In the manuscript notes in his own copy in
the Bodleian Library he adds an inscription he found at
Wornington, near Peterborough, and draws what he describes as a 'stone trough' (apparently a stone coffin) with the
inscription on one of the sloping faces of the lid, though all he
shows of that is the fragmentary 'PVR ESTE . . . FNE ICISVI : WS
. . . TRESPASSANZ PRE . . .'[17]

He states that two of the inscriptions he recorded were filled with lead, which is rather unusual and, if he is to be trusted, may add another factor to our estimate of these early inscriptions. One is at Ancaster, where 'On a stone laid upon the church wall I read this inscription in large letters of lead melted into the cavitys. PRIEZ : PVR : LE : ALME : SIRE : JOHN : COLMAD : CHIVALER (Pray for the soul of Sir John Colmad, Knight)' (*Ic*, p 81); and the other, mentioned in a note in the Bodleian copy, is a curious slab at Belvoir Priory, Leicestershire. Stukeley notes that in 1726 he 'saw the Tombston of this Robert now dug up, in a stable where was the Priory chappel. ROBERT DE TODĒI LE FV̄DEVR! [Robert de Todeni, the Founder] wrote in large letters with lead cast in them, 'he came in with W^m the Conq^r'.[18] Rather surprisingly Robert de Tounei (which is the correct reading) really did come over with Duke William, but the inscription, of course, was not made till the early fourteenth century. It was dug up again in 1792, when Gough saw it and also commented on traces of lead in the letters, and yet again in 1923. It is now in Belvoir Castle.[19]

Stukeley's only illustration of a brass in the *Itinerarium* is a very poor drawing of Bishop Smith's brass in Lincoln. As a source he cites Browne Willis, who must in turn have taken the drawing from Sanderson, since the original is supposed to have been destroyed by *'Cromwelli flagitiosus grex'* in 1654. Another Stukeley drawing of a brass shows the remarkable double palimpsest from Great Stukeley, Huntingdonshire.[20] The drawing is much better than that of the Smith brass, and when the original indent was found about 1900, it was instantly recognised. As the brass figure, which survived in Stukeley's time, was in fact loose and in danger of being sold, he appropriated it and set it up in his summer house.

Itineraries as a method of recording antiquities did not really survive the eighteenth century, though of course chance references to brasses in accounts of travels may be of great value. Cobbett makes only one reference to a brass, among his notes on turnips in *Rural Rides*, but it was the only record of the tiny inscription to Queen Catherine of Aragon until his reference was followed up and the original brass discovered.[21]

HERALDIC VISITATIONS

An important group of early sources for lost brasses is the Heralds' Visitations. It was a function of the Officers of Arms to tour the country ensuring that no one was using coats of arms to which they were not entitled, and making them prove their title to arms by genealogical research. Genealogy was considered a subject of the highest importance, and it is typical of the age that Queen Elizabeth's most cogent reason for prohibiting the destruction of tombs was that they were necessary as proofs of genealogy or heraldry. With parish registers inadequate or non-existent, the inscriptions and heraldry on tombs were often the only solid evidence to support a family's claim to arms, and so the heralds were instructed to copy down all inscriptions and coats of arms displayed on tombs in all churches. Sir William Dugdale wrote to an Ulster King at Arms in the late seventeenth century recommending, 'If the person thus entring his descent, can make out his pedigree, by any Aunthentique evidence for more descents than the memory of any man living can reach: it will be proper to register the same with a Voucher of those Authorities, viz[t] . . . Monumentall Inscriptions, or what else may be relyed upon, as of Creditt.'[22] From this we see that inscriptions on brasses were considered reliable evidence, to be collected as part of the process of proving a person's 'descent' or genealogy. Needless to say the heralds did not achieve anything like a complete record of arms and inscriptions in churches, for visitations were irregular and seldom complete, and most heralds recorded no more than the coat of arms and a family tree without copying out the evidence. However, the visitations do provide us with quite a lot of useful information.

An early visitation was that made in 1530 of St Paul's Cathedral and seventeen City churches.[23] This was not the normal type of visitation of families to check their right to bear arms, but a 'visitation of burials' to ensure that the heraldry displayed on tombs was correct. In the process the herald took notes on the tombs, such as this from St Paul's:

> Without the Qwer at the upper ynd of the cherge, a lytill frome the scryne of Saincte Earcnolde, lyth a Knyght of the Order of the Garter, with the Garter abutte his Leke; and on hym a fayre long Slatte-Ston wherin he lyghe pykter in brasse; and on the said Ston in dyvers places, the Garter sett and grave in the said metall of brasse; whos name ys ther ingraven. And calld Mons[r] Aleyn Burschate: but there ys maid ther no memory what tyme nor what Dayte, he was ther beryed; but hyt schuld be the daye of Henry the Vth of whos sooll Jhesu have merce.

Although several brasses from Old St Paul's are well known, by chance this one is not adequately described in any other source.

A report of a later visitation-'The gatherings of Oxfordsher A[0] Dom 1574'[24] in the Bodleian Library-consists mostly of small drawings or 'tricks' of shields, drawn indiscriminately from stone, brass and glass, in churches and manor houses. Usually the only notes that are included are family names, but often it can be deduced that the shields come from brasses, and in several places the heraldry missing from surviving brasses can be reconstructed from them. Occasionally, however, the notes specify that the arms come off tombs, and in a few cases give epitaphs or extracts from epitaphs: for instance, 'In Trinitye Colidge [old Durham College] on a stone. Sir Henre hansport esqu for ye bodye to kyng henry the vij[th] & constable of the castell of Duram ob xx[th] of July 1497.' Brasses at Ewelme and Tackley are briefly described, and the description for a brass at North Aston reads, 'a man in armour & a woman in a bursons robe very ancint io quo ann p alicia uxor eius ob 1416'.

More typical of visitation reports is that of the 1634 Visitation of Sussex.[25] This consists almost entirely of shields of arms and brief pedigrees, but notes scattered apparently at random give us the missing heraldry of some surviving brasses and provide the only record of the name and date of a brass for which a very worn and indistinct indent survives at Steyning: 'On a Gravestone these Armes and inscription . . . Pray for the soules of Michell Fownefeild and Joane his wife wch Michell deceased the 24 daie of Nouemb^r A^0 Dni M. V. C viij on whose soules Jesus have mercie.'

As well as the official visitations, the heralds were often commissioned to compile elaborate pedigrees for particular families; the fair copies of several of these include drawings of tombs and brasses. Gough describes one drawn up at considerable expense for the Howard family in the reign of Charles I by Henry Lilly, Rouge Dragon Pursuivant.[26] This includes drawings of two important brasses to Thomas, second Duke of Norfolk, and his Duchess, both now lost. A very important and remarkable brass at Burton Agnes, Yorkshire, is known to us only from a drawing by Francis Thynne, Lancaster Herald, on a similar pedigree dated 1604. If Thynne is to be trusted, the brass showed a cross-legged armoured figure, with an inscription in Lombardic letters running over an arch above him, and two angels holding a shield among stars at the top.[27] It commemorates Sir Roger Somerville, 1336, and is useful as a dated example in the sequence of early military brasses.

Unfortunately very few of these heraldic documents have been published or are readily accessible. Many of the most interesting pedigrees are still in private possession, and most of the rest of the material is in the College of Arms. There are copies of several visitations, however, in the British Museum and Bodleian Library.

One source, which has been published with many drawings in facsimile, is a rough notebook compiled by John Philpot, Somerset Herald, consisting of church notes taken between 1613 and 1642, evidently in the course of visitations.[28] There is a large number of sketches of kneeling figures in tabards or mantles showing their coats of arms, though it is never quite clear whether these are taken from brasses or stained glass, except of course where the brass survives, in which case the notes are superfluous. Philipot includes a sketch of the brass of the Countess of Atholl at Ashford, but it is so poor that one would be at a loss to reconstruct the original design from it and the surviving fragments. The manuscript is typical of these heraldic church notes, though in fact it adds comparatively little to our knowledge.

A factor that must always be borne in mind when dealing with notes made by heralds is that their commission and interests were heraldic and genealogical, not artistic. In the vast majority of cases all they record is the inscription and coat of arms on a brass, without mentioning the existence of figures, canopies, saints and other features.

THE FIRST ANTIQUARIES

As a result of the visitations, the heralds were among the first to take a real interest in brasses for their own sake. Their professional recording of heraldry and inscriptions on tombs soon aroused an interest in tombs and brasses in general, and their widening interests led to the first thorough antiquarian works.

The most famous of the early herald antiquaries was Sir William Camden, 1551-1623, Clarenceux King of Arms, who published his famous *Britannia* in 1586. This is a topographical description by counties, giving a brief history of each county with notes on the geography and natural history, followed by a gazetteer of places of interest with descriptions of various antiquities and monuments up to his own time. The work is very short, considering its scope, but it is an important milestone as the first attempt to describe monuments consistently. References to brasses are in fact tantalisingly few, though Camden is the only source for an inscription at Arundel, to Henry Fitzalan, 1579-80; and he sketches an early indent in Cornwall and gives a few other useful notes; but on the whole he is more admirable as a pioneer than as a source for research.[29]

Contemporary with Camden was John Stow, 1525-1605, who published *A Survey of London* in 1598.[30] This is a very methodical account of London, ward by ward, as it was before the fire of 1666, and it includes burial lists for all the churches, including the monasteries dissolved before his time. Some are simply lists of names, but these have several times proved useful for identifying the original locations of brasses re-used in other parts of the country. For instance, the reverse of the Waterperry brass, to Simon Kemp, was finally tracked down to Holy Trinity Priory, Aldgate, by Stow's burial list. In other cases he expands a little and mentions whether tombs have brasses or not, with brief descriptions such as 'John Shirley, esquire, and Margaret his wife, having their pictures of brass, in the habit of pilgrims, on a fair flat stone with an epitaph . . .' in St Bartholemew the Less. For some he transcribes the epitaphs in full, such as this to Thomas Knowles, in St Anthony's, Budge Row:

Here lies graven under this stone,
Thomas Knowles both flesh and bone;
Grocer and alderman, yeares fortie
Shiriffe and twice maior truly.
And for he should not lie alone,
Here lieth with him his good wife Joan.
They were togither sixtie yeare,
And nineteen children they had in feere.

The record is, of course, all the more valuable as most of the churches and monuments he describes were swept away in the fire, but already much was lost by his time, and several times he notes 'monuments of the dead in this church defaced.'

The greatest and most important of pre-Civil War writers on brasses was John Weever, who published the first specialist book, *Ancient Funerall Monuments*, in 1631. The first half of

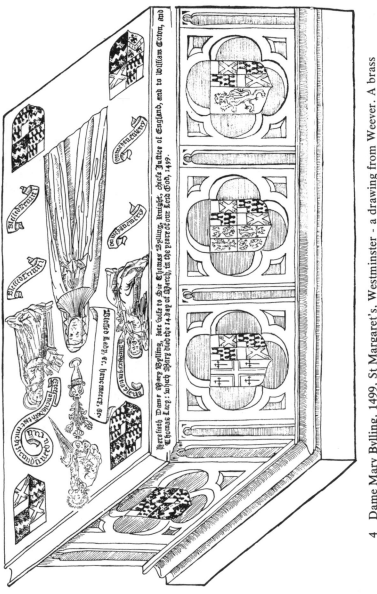

4 Dame Mary Bylling, 1499, St Margaret's, Westminster - a drawing from Weever. A brass on an altar tomb, with the Annunciation

the book is a fascinating account of tombs, graves and epitaphs in general, including much useful material already quoted about the destruction of brasses in the sixteenth century. This is illustrated by the second half, which is a very thorough gazetteer of tombs, nearly all brasses, in the dioceses of London, Norwich, Canterbury and Rochester-in fact the richest areas for brasses. Weever copies the inscriptions and heraldry, but, in common with most of his contemporaries, often neglects to mention whether there are any figures, and rarely describes them. On the whole the inscriptions are not to be taken as literal transcripts of the brasses, for he is not ashamed to alter the spelling, expand some abbreviations and introduce others, and he very often gives the dates in Arabic numerals where they must have been in Roman. As a source for reconstructing lost or damaged brasses, however, he is invaluable.

He provides only a very few illustrations, but by chance they are all of brasses since destroyed. He includes engravings of two fine brasses from St Margaret's, Westminster, which we know were sold off at 3d or 4d a pound in 1644: one shows a widow, Dame Mary Bylling, 1499, under a group representing the Annunciation (Fig 4), and the other shows one of her husbands kneeling at a prie-dieu with fifteen children crowded behind him, an early example of what was to become a common type (*AFM*, 494-5). Another engraving shows Sir Richard Dering and two wives, c 1470, at Pluckley, Kent, with a colt lying at his feet and a lion at those of one of his wives.

Weever's transcripts of epitaphs have frequently been found useful for filling in the gaps in inscriptions now mutilated. The huge brass of Abbot Stoke, 1451, in St Alban's, is now so mutilated that the inscription is incomprehensible without the missing lines which Weever provides. Often, however, he shows the brasses already severely damaged, as at Cobham, Kent, where the Cobham family brasses remained in the state Weever found them until the nineteenth-century restorations. In other churches the brasses have been swept away, as at St Peter's church in St Albans, which seems to have had a very remarkable collection.

Not all Weever's notes were from his own observation, and variations in accuracy may be due to a variety of transcribers. In one case he says that he is including epitaphs and inscriptions collected by Robert Treswell, Somerset Herald, about 1590, 'of which few or none are to be found at the present time'. (*AFM,* 693). His coverage of the areas selected, though not complete, is remarkably thorough, and the extent of his coverage has never been equalled, though more up-to-date lists and transcripts of inscriptions exist for most of the counties covered.

The practice of copying epitaphs spread among antiquaries, and there are a number of very useful documents recording brasses and epitaphs from individual churches or areas. Sir Edward Dering did much useful work in Kent, and several of his sketches and notes were published by R. H. d'Elboux. From them a solitary figure of a daughter surviving at East Langdon could be identified as the only remnant of a brass to Martha Master, with three children.[31]

The two most important single churches to have lost brasses during the Commonwealth are of course York and Lincoln Minsters, and it is fortunate that diligent antiquaries had copied the epitaphs from both before the damage was done. At Lincoln drawings were made of most of the brasses by Robert Sanderson, 1587-1663, afterwards Bishop of Lincoln, and Sir William Dugdale, and the inscriptions were preserved for 150 brasses, seven of which were attributed to the thirteenth century. This record was made only 13 years before the brasses were taken.

Similarly, all the epitaphs for York are preserved in a manuscript compiled by Roger Dodsworth in 1618.[32] He gives 157 epitaphs, mentioning that the vast majority of them are brasses. Normally he does no more than transcribe the inscription and trick the heraldry, but occasionally he gives us some idea of the design of the brass:

About ye brasse tombe in the iron grate on ye suthe by y^e
Clarke. hauing a wound in his head. Hic requiescit corpus
Willielmi Languetona quondam Decani Eboraci qui objit die
sci Swithuni anno dni milessimo ducen: tesimo septuagesimo
nono. Cuius anima sit cum Deo. Note yat yis Willm Langton
was slayne by a man in armor kneeling att masse, as appeareth
by ye story depicted in ye glasse window adjoininge.

It appears that Dodsworth was confused by a window
depicting the martyrdom of St Thomas, but it would be
interesting to know what he meant by a 'wound in his head' on
the brass. A brass of 1279 would, of course, be exceptional
but by no means impossible, though it may well have been
engraved several years later.

Many of the York brasses were already mutilated by Dodsworth's time. Evidently the inscription had already gone from
Archbishop Greenfield's brass of 1315, as he does not
mention it. Others he says are mutilated, such as 'the picture
of a man in brasse it taken away, are thes wordes in divers
places Jesu fili dei miserere tui Ranulphi'.

Dodsworth also copied inscriptions from other parts of
Yorkshire, and collected much of the material for Dugdale's
Monasticon. Sir William Dugdale, 1605-80, Garter King at
Arms, was one of the most important antiquaries of the seven-
teenth century. His largest work, the *Monasticon
Anglicanum*, does not contain much about brasses, but both
his *Antiquities of Warwickshire* (1656) and *History of St
Paul's* (1658) contain many engravings of brasses. For
Warwickshire, not a county rich in brasses, he preserves
engravings of about fifteen now lost. More important, however, are the sixteen engravings of brasses in Old St Paul's by
the Bohemian Wenceslaus Hollar. Besides those illustrated
Dugdale gives the inscriptions of about twenty other brasses,
all of which were either destroyed in the fire of 1666 or, more
likely, salvaged and sold afterwards. The number of brasses
recorded by Dugdale is small compared to York or Lincoln,
and we know from other sources that his list was not com-

5 Judge Ralph Hengham, 1308, St Paul's Cathedral - a drawing by Hollar from Dugdale. An early brass with separate-letter inscription and the slab powdered with 'devices'

6 Richard Lichfild, Canon, 1496, St Paul's Cathedral - a drawing by Hollar from Dugdale. Two birds holding scrolls flank the indent, possibly for a Virgin and Child

plete, but the ones he illustrates are extremely interesting, and five are unique. There are several bishops and deans, with elaborate vestments and canopies decorated with saints, and a fine early brass to Ralph Hengham, Judge of the King's Bench, 1308. This brass is a good parallel to the surviving slabs at Trotton, Sussex, and Saltwood, Kent, all of which show backgrounds scattered with stars and odd devices, which Hollar sees as little animals. As at Trotton the inscription is in separate letters, and like Saltwood there must have been angels above the canopy, though the drawing shows that the indents were effaced (Figs 5 and 28). Many of the large canopied brasses have been reproduced from Dugdale's illustrations,[33] though there is plenty of interest in some of the smaller brasses, such as that to Richard Lichfield, 1496, with two birds (Fig 6).

POST-RESTORATION ANTIQUARIES

After the Restoration the cult of antiquarianism spread rapidly among the educated gentry. Work became more specialised and more localised. Following the lead of Dugdale in writing histories of particular counties or churches we find Ashmole working on Berkshire, Wood in Oxfordshire, Aubrey covering Wiltshire and Surrey, Gunton dealing with Peterborough Cathedral, and others. Only Dingley among important writers drew his material from a wider area.

Another herald, Elias Ashmole, 1617-92, is chiefly known for his heraldic writings, and for his collection of antiquities, which he bequeathed to Oxford. With regard to brasses, his most important work is his history of Berkshire.[34] In this he copies the epitaphs and heraldry, and occasionally describes the figures, of virtually all the brasses in the county, including nearly 150 that have since been lost. For many he is the only authority, and for others he corroborates the less complete records of others, or explains surviving indents. Most of the damage to brasses must have already been done before his time, but the high number lost since shows how important his work was. At Windsor he lists twenty-two lost brasses, including eleven showing Canons of the Order of the Garter, and at St Lawrence, Reading, fourteen, of which only four survive.

Across the river Anthony Wood was even more thorough in recording brasses in Oxfordshire. He collected material for a history of both University and City, including detailed descriptions of all the churches and chapels, and records of the brasses in them. He also covered most of the parish churches of Oxfordshire, so that his collection in its entirety is of unparalleled value, covering as it does the area most densely populated by surviving brasses.[35] The history of the University was published in 1674, but to his great disgust in Latin.

As well as recording all the monuments in college chapels surviving in his time, he evidently had access to various pre-Civil War records, as he is able to list several brasses lost before his time, including twenty-five plundered from New College Cloisters when they were requisitioned as an ammunition dump in 1643. He gives more detail about the brasses than many of his contemporaries, usually stating whether there was a figure, and of what type, 'the effigies of a young man, kneeling' or 'the effigies of a man in a gown', and occasionally giving more information. A very curious indent that survives in New College is quite incomprehensible until it is compared with Wood's description: 'two hands issuing out of the clouds, holding over his head a doctoral cap, (round, and somewhat steepled) such as was worn by Theologists in his time.'

More interesting, though rather disorganised, are the unfinished notes for his history of the city. Most of the material on brasses is collected in one section, but some appears in his jottings on individual churches and religious houses. Many brasses were already lost by his time: he can tell us nothing about most of the indents in Christ Church or St Mary's, but others he gives from earlier sources. For instance, when describing the brasses of St Martin's Church, he three times referred obliquely to Miles Windsore (fl 1574) as 'an obscure note', 'my curious researches' or 'my obscure oracle', who supplied the inscriptions, all of which were lost possibly following the Ordinance of 1644. In these city notes he often expands into quite elaborate descriptions of the brasses, such as this from St Mary Magdalen's:

> The pictures of a man & woman kneeling on either side of the picture of God sitting in a chaire, holding y^t of Christ hanging on the crosse, between his leggs, with ye picture of a dove (representing the holy ghost) on his hand. Behind the man was engraven ye picture of St Katherine mediating to God for him & behind the woman the picture of St Brigit doing the like for her & und' all this inscription: Orate pro animabus Johannis Havelde et Johanne uxoris ejus, qui quidem Johannes obiit xviii Octobris anno Dom MCCCC LXXXXVIII. Quorum animabus ppitietur deus, Amen.

This account is corroborated by Symonds, who gives the wording of the scrolls, and by a remarkable chance by the recent discovery of a rubbing made in 1812, when the brass was loose and mutilated. Wood's description is accurate, though he obviously took no trouble to reproduce the inscription exactly (frontispiece).

Another great county historian was John Aubrey, 1626-97, who compiled great collections for Wiltshire and Surrey in the late seventeenth century. Neither have been properly edited and published, though an edition of the Surrey material is in progress. Aubrey was catholic in his interests, which included much natural history and folklore, with a wide range of antiquarian subjects, but he records several brasses since lost from the two counties, and includes a few drawings. Two are reproduced in Kite's *Wiltshire,* one being from Hilmerton, a brass to a vicar, John Wylkys, with a unique shield-shaped plate bearing a chalice. A great many more from Surrey are preserved only in Aubrey's notes, but most of these are collated in Mill Stephenson's *Surrey,* though from an inferior text. Brasses were still being lost as Aubrey wrote, since he notes at Burstow: 'Desire Sir Edwarde Bishe to returne to this church ye inscription in Brasse, that was in the chancell-chest.'[36] He strayed over the border into Sussex in 1692, and in three pages of the manuscript records two brasses not otherwise known from Slinfold-one 'brasse on marble' to John Bradbrige and wife, 1503, with the 'figure of ye man w^t gowne and powres' and a 'lady dresst like ye Queene'.[37]

The most remarkable of the late seventeenth-century antiquaries was Thomas Dingley or Dineley, who died in 1695. He seems to have come originally from Herefordshire and been a lawyer of sorts, though he travelled widely in England and abroad. His principal work is a curious document entitled *An Historie from Marble,* probably finished about 1685.[38] Basically it is a collection of sketches and notes on tombs, especially brasses, though the author breaks off from time to time into such digressions as a delightful drawing of a dragon or a poem in praise of cider. The bulk of his material comes from the Midlands, between Oxford and Hereford, though there is quite a lot from London, including sketches of some of the brasses in Old St Paul's. On the whole the drawings are atrocious, though he was evidently aware of his incapacity to draw figures, and frequently draws only the shields, scrolls and inscriptions. When he does draw figures, they are unrecognisable, for instance, his sketch purporting to be the well-known brass of Bishop Trellick at Hereford has no relation to the original at all-but he makes up for this by accurate recording of inscriptions and heraldry, and descriptions of the figures and canopies. His text can be rather difficult to unravel, as the notes are mixed up with the drawings (including totally irrelevant ones), but it is usually possible to reconstruct what he must have seen.

Some of his most useful notes and sketches are of the brasses in All Saints', Oxford, before they were destroyed in 1701. The inscriptions are mostly duplicated in Wood, but

Dingley preserved sketches of four of the brasses from which it was possible to identify the indents when they were discovered in 1973.[39]

The increase in amateur epitaph collecting in the late seventeenth century was probably in part due to the fact that the Civil War had drawn people's attention to the amount of damage that could be done to brasses (though, as we have seen, it was by no means the most destructive period), and they considered the preservation of the remaining epitaphs a matter of urgency lest civil war break out again. After the usurpation of William of Orange the situation may have appeared more stable, and this may account for the waning of enthusiasm, since in the last years of the seventeenth century and the first half of the eighteenth very much less work was done.

Professor Piggott has drawn a distinction between the seventeenth-century 'Royal Society' antiquaries and the eighteenth-century romantics. The former were more scientific observers, collecting the raw materials for objective history, and, in the tradition of the heralds, treating the inscriptions and heraldry as more important than the figures. In the eighteenth century interest swung to the aesthetic side: costumes, architectural details, styles and draughtsmanship became paramount, and inscriptions were often ignored altogether.

THE ROMANTIC ANTIQUARIES

In the first half of the eighteenth century there were few writers of any real importance for the study of brasses. Stukeley, who in person marks the change from scientist to romantic, has already been mentioned. Hearne, Dart and Drake give us some information, but are not really interested in brasses. Rawlinson and Browne Willis are the only great epitaph collectors, and they do not often expand on earlier work.

Thomas Hearne, 1678-1735, left a vast collection of

material of miscellaneous antiquarian interest, mostly relating to Oxfordshire and Berkshire.[40] His collections of epitaphs are of small value, since they are mostly copied from Wood and Ashmole, though he has a few original discoveries. Perhaps the most curious and tenuous way in which the wording of an inscription has been preserved is given in his account of St Cross Church, Oxford:

> In the South Wall of the Church was formerly fix'd a Brass Plate, that hath been taken down for some Years. When 'twas first took down, the Clarke apprehending that 'twould be quite lost took care to have the Inscription upon it preserved by having it written at the End of a Common Prayer Book now lying in the Church, in which I saw it, & have transcrib'd it from thence . . .

Primarily, however, Hearne was a Romanist, and brasses were not one of his major interests. More information can be gathered from the collections of Richard Rawlinson, 1690-1755, who produced a large number of monographs on individual cities, cathedrals and churches, usually published anonymously by E. Curll of Fleet Street. He also left extensive manuscript collections, including transcripts of epitaphs. His collections for Oxfordshire were collated with the published versions of Wood's notes, from which it is clear that he makes few additions from his own observation.

Similar work was done by Browne Willis, 1682-1760, who published a large collection of cathedral surveys, and a history of Buckinghamshire.[41] The cathedral surveys are extremely useful in that they collect all the available evidence for monuments, including those lost before his time. In his lists of cathedral officials he includes their monuments, not only in their own cathedrals but wherever else they might be buried, even as far as the English College at Rome. He also takes notice of indents, and makes valiant efforts to identify them. For instance at Lichfield:

Gravestones robbed of their Brass Inscriptions. These were no less than sixty seven; but as they have been divers of them remov'd from Place to Place, on new paving the Church, there is no ascertaining to whom they belonged: Tho' it is plain four of them belonged to Bishops, as is apparent by the Impression of the Mitre and Crosier on the Stones. One of these was doubtless for Bishop *Halse* [1490] another Bishop *Boler's*, [1459] a third Bishop *Burghill's* [1414] and the fourth probably for Bishop *Close* [1452]. These seem to have been all of them spoiled of their Brasses about the Beginning of Queen *Elizabeth's* Reign . . .[42]

Willis' conjectures are informed by researches revealing, for instance, that Bishop Burghill ordered a brass in his will. His Buckinghamshire collections are also very useful, and can be cited to identify brasses and indents in that county.

A more detailed work on a single church is F. Drake's *Eboracum or the History and Antiquities of the City of York*, 1736. This devotes a large section to the brasses and monuments of the Cathedral, though Drake's information on inscriptions is almost entirely drawn from Dodsworth. He includes several engravings, purporting to be of brasses, but it is clear that they are sheer phantasies on his part, since the engraving of the surviving brass of Archbishop Greenfield bears no resemblance to the original, and the full page engraving of Archdeacon Dalby's brass is quite inconceivable as a brass supposed to date from the early sixteenth century.

In contrast to this, J. Dart's *Westmonasterium* of 1742 includes six very fine and accurate engravings of brasses, done at the beginning of a period, stretching to the end of the century, during which engraving was to develop into a real art form. Four of the brasses he engraves survive, though one is badly mutilated. One of the others is the curious and unique brass of Thomas Woodstock, Duke of Gloucester, son of Edward III; this showed the Duke in his Garter robes in the centre, under a Trinity flanked by two saints, and completely surrounded by his relations, with the King at the top and the

101

Duchess at the bottom, all held together by very unusual canopy work.[43] Dart also records much useful information about the other brasses in Westminster Abbey, including copies of lost inscriptions.

In the second half of the eighteenth century antiquarianism flourished again, and for the first time serious study was given to the designs of brasses. The first rubbings and impressions were made, as were the first attempts to examine styles, costume and armour. The oldest rubbing now known to survive was probably made in March 1754 by Thomas Martin in St Peter's, Kirkley, near Lowestoft.[44] It shows only a small sixteenth-century inscription, but it very unlikely that it was Martin's only rubbing, and probably many rubbings were being made by different antiquaries from about 1750 onwards, though little survives earlier than 1780.

The Regency was the heyday of the romantic antiquarian, the date of many of the best county histories, and the best period of the *Gentleman's Magazine,* the forum for amateur antiquarians from 1731 to 1868. The central character in much of this was John Nichols, 1745-1826, who as editor of the *Gentleman's Magazine* received antiquarian correspondence, and appears to have been the leader of a group of scholars, including Richard Gough and John Carter. These three collaborated on their respective *magna opera*: Nichols's *History of Leicestershire,* 1795-1809, by far the largest and best of the county histories; Carter's *Specimens of Ancient Architecture,* 1825, a major factor in the Gothic Revival; and, most important of all for brasses, Gough's *Sepulchral Monuments,* 1786-1802. Circling round them was a group of skilled antiquarian draughtsmen and engravers, of whom the most important were Schnebbelie; James Basire, father, son and grandson; and John Buckler and son. Many others corresponded with the *Gentleman's Magazine,* submitting accounts and drawings of brasses, as well as covering an amazingly wide range of antiquarian and naturalist subjects.

The various county histories written about this time contain more useful information, not only directly about brasses themselves but also on family histories and genealogies that help to date many brasses and indents. These histories vary greatly in content: for instance, Lysons's *Environs of London* contains very little of use to chalcologists, whereas Burrell's unfinished Sussex notes are an invaluable source for lost brasses.

Nichols's *Leicestershire* covers a county rich in incised slabs but on the whole poor in brasses. Nichols records both, and illustrates a large proportion. Many of the drawings of incised slabs were reproduced by Mr Greenhill in *The Incised Slabs of Leicestershire and Rutland,* which shows how variable was the quality of Nichols's draughtsmen. However, it is usually possible to extrapolate back from them to a reasonable reconstruction of what the originals must have been like. Of brasses, Nichols illustrates twenty-seven now surviving and fourteen now lost from Leicestershire, as well as some from other counties commemorating Leicestershire families. These lost brasses include some large and fine examples, such as a large brass to Sir Thomas and Isabel Chaworth, 1458, at Launde Abbey, and an unusual brass of a priest giving a blessing while holding the chalice and Host, at Stanford. In addition to brasses, Nichols included indents in his survey, and has preserved drawings of unusual indents such as that at Belgrave, showing two crosses with elongated octofoil heads separated by rows of stars, with an inscription in separate letters to Roger and Susanna de Belgrave, whom he dates to 1278. The most impressive illustration in the book is a full-size print of a large and remarkable inscription from Leatheringham, Suffolk, which was actually in Nichols's possession. Sadly, the inscription is now lost, but the impressions provided by Nichols are prints off the surface of the brass, for it was treated as if it were a copper plate intended for printing. The result of course is that the writing is reversed, but the accuracy of the print outweighs this disadvantage.[45]

This method of reproducing brasses by making prints off

the surface seems to have been fairly widely practised among antiquaries in the latter half of the eighteenth century. Despite the obvious disadvantages of its inconvenience when dealing with brasses still in situ (it must have been impossible to print mural brasses in this way), the method has the advantages of absolute accuracy and clarity. Since not even a thickness of paper separates the original from the print, the slightest or most worn engraving is reproduced. The most famous exponents of the art were Craven Ord and Sir John Cullum, who made a sizeable collection of impressions off brasses mainly from East Anglia and the south Midlands. Of these about 240 are now in the British Museum.[46] The majority were made in 1779-80, and the others within a few years. Several reproduce brasses that are now lost, and as full-size prints are, of course, perfect records. The most important are those from Ingham and King's Lynn, where the brasses were stolen shortly after 1800. One of those from King's Lynn is the male figure only of a large Flemish brass, similar to those surviving, but apparently then in better condition, to Robert Attelathe, 1376 (see Fig 8). Unfortunately Ord did not copy the wife or canopy, noting 'There is his wife also, but as her Dress did not differ from those in the Quire, I did not take her.' Annoyingly, he very often failed to complete his prints, taking only figures and omitting canopies and other accessories, as well as regularly omitting inscriptions.

Many of Ord's prints, and others done by the same process, were used by Richard Gough and his engravers in preparing material for his *Sepulchral Monuments*.[47] This is perhaps the most important (certainly the largest) book on brasses and monuments. The collected material—notes, drawings and proof plates—is all in the Bodleian Library, where it forms a mine of useful information, including a great deal that was never published. No material later than 1500 was included in the book, though it is clear from the manuscripts and the title of the book that Gough had intended to continue till the seventeenth century.

Bound into the first volume of Part II are a number of direct prints of brasses, which, like the example included by Nichols, came from the breaking up of Leatheringham Church. They consist of two mutilated inscriptions, four shields and a figure, of which only the figure and one shield survive. These loose Leateringham brasses seem to have passed between Gough and Nichols until some at least settled in the Bodleian, whence the surviving plates were recently returned to Leatheringham.

The majority of the engravings with which the book is illustrated were drawn for Gough by Schnebbelie and John Carter, and engraved by Basire, though others are signed by Cook, J. Johnson, S. H. Grimm, Tynson, G. Vertue, 'Caroline Basire, now Langdon' and others. Some were drawn by Basire's apprentice, William Blake. Some of the poorer examples are not signed, like the plate showing a Style 'C' knight and wife, from Walpole St Peter, Norfolk (Fig 7). Many of the engravings were obviously prepared from impressions off the surface of the brass, as they are reversed, with the sword appearing on the wrong side of the figure. A few of these impressions are preserved among the material in the Bodleian, while others are now with the Craven Ord collection in the British Museum. Gough's engraving of the lost Attelathe brass from King's Lynn is almost certainly copied from Ord's impression (Fig 8). The other engravings were made from pencil drawings and ordinary rubbings, of which many are in the Bodleian. The best of these rubbings were done by Schnebbelie, who seems normally to have used a large block of plombagine or graphite, though some were done with pencil. One of the finest of these is a complete rubbing of the very large brass of Walter Coney, 1479, also from King's Lynn, showing the rather unusual canopy, scrolls and other parts, where Ord only took an impression of the figure. Many other rubbings show brasses now lost of which no other accurate representations survive.

Gough and his circle were concerned with brasses not

7 (*left*) Sir Ralph and Maud Rochford, 1390, Walpole St Peter, Norfolk. This engraving from Gough shows Style 'C' effigies under the indents for a double canopy

8 (*right*) Robert Attelathe, 1376, St Margaret's, King's Lynn, Norfolk - an engraving from Gough after a print by Ord. A fine Flemish figure, part of a very large composition

106

simply as historical records, like the earlier antiquaries, but as works of art. Gothic art was beginning to be appreciated for its own sake. In dealing with the Braunch brass at King's Lynn, one of the surviving Flemish plates, he is able to use the language of artistic criticism, and is quite out of sympathy with the patient epitaph collectors (I, 115):

> In the choir of St Margaret's church at *Lynne* is a brass plate so highly finished, and so exquisitely embellished, that one knows not what censure to pass on those tasteless Topographers who content them selves with a hasty transcript of its epitaph. But since the discernment and industry of my two friends before-mentioned [Ord and Cullum] have rescued it from future obscurity, by taking off a fac simile, I shall contribute my endeavours to secure it immortality by the accurate engraving made of it by Mr Carter, on a scale reduced to the proportion of this work. This admirable brass, the exertion of some Cellini of the 14th century, is the monument of a burgess of one of our most commercial and opulent boroughs.

Gough was concerned to illustrate brasses in their entirety, and with any stonework or architectural settings they might have. He arranges his material chronologically, and on the whole is reasonably accurate in his datings, though there are some startling errors. The bulk of material is vast, for he had friends and agents all over the country sending in notes, descriptions and transcripts; and he includes brasses from almost every county in England, as well as noting several from other countries. Among the manuscript material are letters from many sources, enclosing sketches or notes, often evidently in answer to requests from Gough for more accurate detail or delineation. Proof sheets show the care he took to ensure accuracy at least in the inscriptions, though one feels he might have noticed that some of the figures are inside out.

As well as researching in the field, Gough consulted a large number of manuscript and printed sources, which he cites in copious footnotes. The long introductions to the two parts are fascinating accounts of burial customs and monumental art in all countries and at all periods, and include a number of gruesome accounts of the opening of graves and sealed coffins, several of which Gough himself seems to have witnessed. His energy over many years in collecting material, the scope of his work, the richness of his examples and above all the very large number of his illustrations entitle him to recognition as one of the greatest of all chalcologists.

Several of the best of Gough's engravings were drawn and some also engraved by John Carter (1748-1817). He thought of himself primarily as an architect, and his largest works are *Specimens of Gothic Architecture and Ancient Buildings in England,* and *Views of Ancient Buildings in England,* though he also wrote on sculpture, painting, and on costume (which he illustrated partly from brasses). As one of Gough's collaborators he gave Gough the benefit of his work on brasses and tombs, though he included a token few in *Gothic Architecture.* He was a regular correspondent to the *Gentleman's Magazine,* signing his reports 'An Architect'; he commented on antiquities, and furiously denounced official indifference, damage and neglect of ancient monuments.

Many other contributors to the *Gentleman's Magazine* give us useful information about brasses, though the convention of anonymity hides many of their identities. Several lost brasses are illustrated, from drawings of varying quality, and it seems to have been a common pastime for an enthusiast to write up the monuments in a church or two and send a report to Dr Urban. These reports are widely scattered throughout more than 100 years of issues, though the bulk of the most useful notes appear during the Regency. All these are collected in the topographical volumes of the Gentleman's Magazine Library (1891-1902), in which, however, the illustrations are not reproduced. The *Magazine* should be treated with some caution, as its readers were not above perpetrating hoaxes: for example, someone calling himself 'Verus' wrote a totally spurious account of four brasses he claimed to have discovered in St Mary the Virgin's, Oxford, probably as an undergraduate joke.[48]

Antiquarianism was not confined to gentlemen. A large amount of very useful material recently acquired by the Bodleian Library was compiled by an ironmonger, Henry Hinton, and his friend, an apothecary's apprentice, James Hunt. Their project was to write histories of the two counties of Oxford and Berkshire, and for this they collected notes, documents, anecdotes, drawings, engravings and, above all, brass-rubbings. Their collection, now the oldest that is in any way complete for the area it covers, has rubbings of nearly every brass in the two counties. As well as taking rubbings, they made careful notes of the position of the brass in its church, its condition, its arrangement if not clear on the rubbing, and often historical or biographical details. Several of the rubbings show indents, and in addition there are many drawings of indents in the accompanying notebooks (Plate 4a). For each church they visited they copied out Ashmole's or Wood's notes, annotated them, and added details of brasses and indents not mentioned in them. Unfortunately the work was never finished, and the material remains scattered among a large number of notebooks.[49]

The rubbings were mostly made between 1795 and 1820, and all except one or two impressions are true rubbings, made with graphite or blackened leather. None were made for their own sake, but only as aids for making scale drawings for publication in the proposed histories. No care, therefore, was taken to keep the rubbings in good condition once they had been copied, and most of those done on more than one sheet of paper were never assembled. Often in fact they used both sides of the same sheet of paper, or even made one rubbing over the top of another. To prepare the illustration in Plate 1b it was necessary to assemble tracings of both sides of two sheets of paper, and make up a slight gap where supposedly adjacent sections did not meet.

Despite these drawbacks, however, the collection is extremely useful, as it shows all the brasses before the nineteenth-century restorations, in their original slabs, or with

109

parts now lost, and it includes several now totally lost. Among these are the only known rubbings of three brasses lost from Marcham, Berkshire, in 1837, one of which is a very fine Style 'B' knight, engraved c1385, for Sir Robert Corbet, 1403 (Plate 1b). Another is the very unusual quadrangular plate from St Mary Magdalen's, Oxford, which was described by Wood. Hinton found this under a pile of rubbish in 1812, and made two rubbings, from which his drawing reproduced as the frontispiece was prepared. Other lost brasses are included among the drawings, such as that of Thomas Bartlet, 1675, from St Ebbe's, which was probably too lightly engraved to rub (Plate 4b). A typical page from the manuscript shows the fragmentary surviving brasses, the indents, and two eighteenth-century inscriptions from Hurley, Berkshire (Plate 4a). Most of the many other indents included have since been effaced or destroyed.

Another antiquary who concentrated on the brasses of a particular county was John Sell Cotman, 1782-1842, who published a magnificent series of engravings of Norfolk and Suffolk brasses in 1819. They were prepared from rubbings and ink impressions, and include many now lost. The plates are large and accurate, but there is very little text, though for the most part the illustrations speak for themselves.

Contemporary with Cotman was Thomas Fisher, 1781-1836, who worked in Bedfordshire and published a large number of accurate drawings of Bedfordshire brasses.[50] He also drew many Kentish brasses and indents, several of which were reproduced by Ralph Griffin.[51] Like Hinton, he was careful to record the relationship of a brass to its slab and any indents there might be. Many of his drawings give enlargements of the figures with an inset drawing of the whole slab, a useful and archaeological approach that is still all too rare.

As the nineteenth century progressed, the number of antiquaries seriously studying brasses increased, and many books of antiquities, county histories and the like included engravings of brasses. They are all indexed in Mill

Stevenson's *List* under the relevant churches. Probably the finest drawings were those in Stothard's *Monumental Effigies,* 1817, though by chance none of those he illustrates have been lost.

VICTORIAN AND MODERN SOURCES

Soon after the accession of Queen Victoria brass-rubbing blossomed into a popular pastime. As far as we know, all previous rubbings had been made by serious scholars, and usually only as models for engraving copper plates. By 1844, however, heelball had been invented, rubbing became much easier and less messy, and the rubbings themselves were appreciated. By 1846 brass-rubbing was becoming a positive menace:

> Now the difficulty is to find the simplest village church, which possesses a brass, where either the smears on the floor do not give token of an ill-managed heelball, or the clerk civilly inquires if you are furnished with paper, or the sexton exhibits his own rubbing, and requests you to buy it, or (in some cases) forbids you, by making your own copy, to infringe on his monopoly. Nay, a class of men are arising who obtain a livelihood by circuitising the country, and making copies of its most famous brasses, and then exposing them for sale.[52]

Plus ça change, plus c'est la même chose!

The result of this, and subsequent 'waves' of brass-rubbing, is that rubbings now exist for virtually every brass in the country, and few have been lost since about 1840 of which at least one rubbing does not survive. Nor can any be lost in the future of which there are not several rubbings in different collections. The collection of the Society of Antiquaries contains reproductions of nearly all brasses lost since the early nineteenth century, all of which are indexed in Mill Stephenson's *List*. The British Museum also has a large collection of rubbings of lost brasses, and there are others in the

Cambridge Museum, the Bodleian Library and elsewhere. Many more must still be unrecognised in private collections or uncatalogued in libraries. From the point of view of scholarship, therefore, recent losses hardly matter, though obviously it would be an advantage to see the originals. It is unfortunate that this coverage was never extended to the Continent, for many fine brasses were destroyed there during the World Wars, and no rubbings or photographs remain to show what they looked like. Two large brasses from the Vischer workshop, for example, disappeared in this way, one from Szamotuly, and the other from the Dominican church at Poznań.

As well as rubbings, a large number of books and articles were produced during the nineteenth century, and some of these are still standard works. Large-plate reproductions of brasses, some now lost, were produced by the Waller brothers, the Cambridge Camden Society, and the Rev Charles Boutell,[53] as well as several privately produced plates, and, towards the end of the century, photo-lithographs.

Nearly every county in England was covered by a local archaeological society, most of which were founded about the middle of the century. Their annual volumes contain many articles and illustrations covering their local brasses. For instance, in Sussex in 1871 the Rev Edward Turner wrote a guide to Sussex brasses, describing them all, but without illustrations. Many brasses have been moved or relaid since his time, and several are lost, though it appears from other sources that often he was relying on memories of his youth in describing brasses in fact lost well before 1871.[54] Some late brasses, thought 'decadent' and therefore ignored during the restorations, were lost after this time, such as one at Heathfield:

A plate in this church bears the following inscription to the memory of the Hero of Gibraltar:—"The Right Honorable George Augustus Elliot, Lord Heathfield . . . died at Aix la Chapelle July 6th 1790 aged 72 years. This plate was part of a

Spanish gun belonging to the floating battery destroyed before
Gibraltar by the deceased Sept' 13ᵗʰ 1782.

Both Universities were active with work on brasses. In 1835
the Oxford University Genealogical and Heraldic Society
(after 1838 the Archaeological Society) began to collect
rubbings of local brasses, a project that was taken over by the
Architectural Society. By 1848 their material was ready for
publication, in the first textbook on brasses, *A Manual for the
Study of Monumental Brasses.*[55] This was compiled by
Herbert Haines, then an undergraduate, and is a remarkably
thorough and scholarly work, including references to a wide
variety of sources and much information on lost brasses and
contemporary losses. Expanded, with the index of brasses
completed, it reappeared in 1861 as Haines's famous *Manual
of Monumental Brasses,* still a standard work.

The Cambridge Camden Society could not match this, but
produced a series of twenty-four large plates of brasses. The
Society, however, was not above composing historical
romances about these brasses, which have misled the unwary
ever since. Not until 1887 did Cambridge become really
active, with the founding of the Cambridge University
Association of Brass Collectors (after 1893 the national
Monumental Brass Society). In 1893 the Oxford society re-
emerged as the university Brass Rubbing Society, of which
Haines's son was the first vice-president. Both societies have
continued to work on brasses ever since, and their two journals contain the bulk of modern scholarship on brasses,
including a very large amount of material on lost brasses.

On the whole the chief use of nineteenth-century and later
written sources is as secondary authorities. A great many of
the earlier sources were reprinted or summarized in nineteenth-century periodicals, particularly in series like that of
the Camden Society. The Dingley manuscript is preserved in
their facsimile edition, and is widely available, though the
original has apparently been destroyed by fire.[56] It will have

113

been noticed that many of the other sources quoted were printed in the nineteenth century, a practice that has the obvious advantages not only of making the text more widely available but also of preserving the originals from continual handling. It is true that many printed transcripts of manuscripts are inaccurate, but the errors are usually minor alterations to spelling or abbreviation. For practical purposes these errors are of small importance, especially when they appear only as mistakes in the text of the antiquary, and not in the original inscription or epitaph.

County journals and 'notes and queries' are the most accessible sources for transcripts or extracts from Churchwardens' accounts, bills of sale and other incidental sources for brasses. They also provide unexpected information in rambling accounts of society excursions, chatty notes about a picturesque church, notes on items shown at meetings and the like.

An important source, liable to be forgotten, is the contribution made by archaeological reports of excavations on church sites. These mostly appear in the relevant county journal or in one of a few national journals, and are of a steadily increasing standard of accuracy. Many sites are excavated just before they are destroyed, and so any remains of brasses cannot be preserved in situ; indents are rarely preserved, and small scraps of brass usually vanish into boxes in museum storerooms. The published report should contain all the necessary information, though unfortunately few such reports have had the advantage of attention by an expert on brasses, with his specialised knowledge.

Other modern sources should be used with caution. The large number of general books on brasses have tended to avoid the problem of lost brasses, and where they touch on them, it is usually in quoting matters of hearsay or tradition. There is a common repertory of examples, usually stemming originally from Haines, and these have often gained in the retelling. Few general books give sources for their material from which the information can be checked. Books or series of articles on the brasses of a particular county are usually more reliable, and usually quote their sources.

In this necessarily brief run-through of documentary sources for lost brasses there has obviously not been room to include them all, nor even to include all the most important. The idea has been to give a representative sample of the various types of source that are available. It will be clear what a great variety there is, and how difficult it would be to collate all possible sources. Even when researching on a limited area or a single town it would be virtually impossible to be sure that all available sources had been consulted, and we can never guarantee that more information will not turn up from some unlikely source.

Notes for this chapter appear on page 187

5

NUMERICAL ANALYSIS

Brasses are now found in greater numbers in England than in
any other part of Europe. The whole number still remaining
here is probably not less than four thousand, and traces of as
many more, which are now destroyed, may be seen (Haines)

When we have collected both archaeological and documentary evidence, we can begin to draw conclusions regard-
ing the numbers and proportions of lost brasses, and to
investigate how typical a sample is in fact provided by the surviving examples. Until now all generalisations about distribution by date, type and location have been based on surviving
examples alone, and it has indeed been the policy of the
Monumental Brass Society for many years to exclude any sort
of numerical analysis on the grounds that surviving examples
are unrepresentative. It will be the aim of this chapter to
investigate how far this is so, and determine whether we would
be justified in pursuing the analysis of brasses before the evidence for lost brasses has been collected for the whole
country.

Topics that will be investigated are the numbers of surviving brasses of each date compared to the number lost, the
number of surviving brasses of each type compared with the
number lost, and the geographical distribution of lost and
surviving brasses, to see if any significant trends can be
picked out, and whether these may legitimately be extrapola-

ted to areas other than those in question. Obviously the ideal is for the whole country to be covered, but figures will not be available for many areas, as the majority of indents and the vast bulk of documents are still uncollated. These investigations, therefore, must be regarded as only preliminary, based as they are on a relatively small sample.

The sample consists of those churches or counties where reasonably thorough surveys have been carried out. These are the city of Oxford; the counties of Sussex, Surrey, Bedfordshire, Huntingdonshire and Berkshire; and the cathedrals of Lincoln, St Albans, St Pauls, York, Oxford and Chichester.[1] Some of these have been more thoroughly surveyed than others, and there are probably omissions-the author will vouch only for Oxford and West Sussex-but in all of them the number of lost brasses recorded is enough to make a fair comparison with those surviving. In many cases, however, there have been heavy losses from monastic churches of which we have no record, and only where the churches survive in use and the indents are preserved, as at St Albans, can we gain an impression of what the brasses of a typical abbey must have been like.

No attempt has been made to cover brasses later than 1700 as no information is available on them except in Oxford and Sussex.

DISTRIBUTION FROM 1260 TO 1700

If the total number of brasses in the areas under consideration be plotted in diagrammatic form, it is possible to see at a glance at what period brasses were produced in the greatest quantities and at what period the numbers declined. By defining the proportion of surviving brasses it becomes possible to compare the profile obtained from surviving brasses alone with that obtained from all known brasses, and to find out whether adding the information on lost brasses in fact makes a significant difference.

In Fig 9 the total of brasses, lost and surviving, is plotted against a time scale for the counties of Bedfordshire, Berkshire, Oxford, Surrey and Sussex. Each column represents one decade, running from 1280 to 1700. The solid portions show surviving brasses, from which we could deduce a gradual increase in the production from very few examples in the first half of the fourteenth century to a peak in the reign of Henry VI, a falling off during the Wars of the Roses, a steep rise under Henry VII, another falling off again in the reign of Henry VIII, a gradual rise from the mid-sixteenth century to a peak of production under Elizabeth and James I, a falling off again at the Civil War and a slight revival at the Restoration. The highest peak comes about 1630, with only a slightly lesser one in 1600, and rather lower still in 1510.

Adding in the lost brasses brings the columns up to their full height, and shows a dramatically different picture. For a start we see brasses beginning slightly earlier, and rising to a considerable peak about 1325 (though these early brasses are notoriously difficult to date). There is a marked decline, apparently a little too early for the Black Death of 1349, then

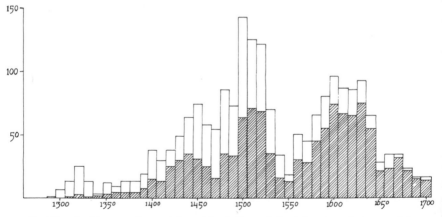

9 The incidence of surviving (shaded) and lost brasses from parish churches in the counties of Bedfordshire, Berkshire, Oxford, Surrey and Sussex over a time scale

118

a rise to a peak under Henry VI as before, a drop for the Wars of the Roses, and a very marked rise under Henry VII, reaching by far the greatest production about 1500. The slump under Henry VIII is even more impressive, but after this lost brasses become a minority, and roughly follow the profile of surviving brasses. The peak of 1600 only reaches 66 per cent of the production of 1500.

The reason for this changed picture is immediately obvious: pre-Reformation brasses were more liable to be destroyed than post-Reformation ones, not for any ideological reason but simply because a significant proportion of the plundering took place in the middle of the sixteenth century. The simple transfer of the peak production from 1600 to 1500 may well be due to this factor alone. The pre-Black Death brasses were even more at risk, since many of them were very delicate—crosses or separate-letter inscriptions—so accidental damage may well have accounted for most of them, besides the fact that they were not properly fastened down, and were therefore easier to steal.

The production of brasses probably reflects economic conditions more than anything else. When times were hard, the production of expensive tombs was abandoned as an unnecessary luxury, and in more prosperous times tombs were often used as status symbols to show off that prosperity. It will be noticed that the very dramatic slump under Henry VIII comes not at the Reformation, nor at the Dissolution of the monasteries, but earlier, soon after 1520, when the king's extravagance and incompetence began to bring about economic depression. Numbers continued to decline after the Reformation partly because the seizure of church property enriched no one but a few courtiers, and partly because the unsettled conditions, the minority of Edward VI, and the serious threat of civil war deterred people from commissioning tombs. Numbers do not pick up until Elizabeth brought relative security and prosperity.

During the two civil wars, 1455-85 and 1641-9, numbers

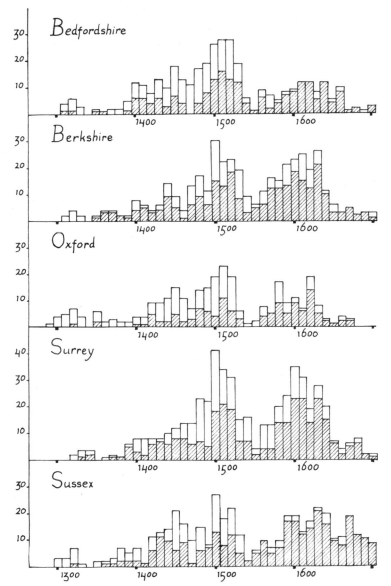

10 The incidence of surviving (shaded) and lost brasses over a time scale, for each county separately. Figures for Huntingdonshire have been added to those for Bedfordshire

decrease. There may well have been more burials, but in times of chaotic communications and general insecurity few were prepared to negotiate the buying of a monument. Brasses never really recovered from the seventeenth-century civil war, as other forms of memorial became popular, and increasingly people turned to stone memorials of various types. After the Wars of the Roses, however, the sudden arrival of the Tudor nouveaux riches brought large numbers of cheap brasses, and the trade reached its greatest peak.

A more puzzling aberration on the chart is the peak reached about 1320, dropping off by 1340. One would expect a drop after the Black Death of 1349, since there was a general economic decline and the country was underpopulated for long after. However, the drop appears to occur before the plague, and numbers pick up again soon after 1350. This may be due to the fact that very few of the early brasses are dated or can be dated accurately from other sources, and so the majority of early indents are given an approximate date of c1325. It is known that this sort of brass was being made from 1299 to at least 1354, so it might well be that many of them should be redated up to 20 years later to produce a peak immediately before the Black Death. Without evidence, however, one cannot do this simply to support a possible interpretation of the course of events, so the early part of the sequence must remain an anomaly.

Examining the areas individually in Fig 10, we see that though they all have the same pattern, there are several anomalies and local characteristics. Berkshire appears to be the most typical county, following the general profile almost exactly. Oxford is similar, but rather surprisingly displays a decline in numbers in and around 1600, when elsewhere brasses were climbing to their second peak. It is noticable that on surviving brasses alone there appears to be only one peak, in 1620, while the lost brasses show an earlier peak in 1580, and a trough between them. There seems no obvious reason for this peculiarity, which may be due to chance.

121

Surrey differs from the other counties in showing no decline at the Wars of the Roses, and, uniquely, an increase in numbers briefly in 1540. The story of Surrey seems to be a gradual rise in importance towards the end of the Middle Ages as a small rural county became increasingly bound up with the life of the capital. The rise in 1540 may well have been due to settlement by Londoners, including the courtiers who had swallowed the wealth of the church.

Huntingdonshire provides too small a sample to be significant on its own, and so the figures have been added to those for Bedfordshire. Together they show a fairly normal pattern up to 1550, and then never recover properly from the mid-sixteenth-century decline. This is odd in an area of which much only became habitable in the seventeenth century, and one can only suppose that here, unusually, is a genuine instance of Protestant feeling against brasses. Both Bedford and Huntingdon were centres of Puritanism, and this may have affected the trade in brasses, which were, after all, literally graven images.

Sussex has a much more jagged profile, but basically follows the normal pattern, though with two unusual peaks in 1630 and 1670. The latter is almost entirely due to the products of a local West Sussex workshop producing large numbers of inscriptions and coffin-plates.

The general pattern, therefore, is fairly consistent, and it is also clear that without a study of lost brasses we would have a very distorted picture. Surviving brasses alone will tell us nothing of the boom in production before the Black Death, and, more importantly, obscure the fact that the greatest quantity of brasses were produced between 1490 and 1520. Although in fact only about a third of the brasses tabulated in the diagrams are lost, they correct the picture to a remarkable extent.

Fig 11 shows the results obtained from the cathedrals and monastic churches combined. Obviously the rate of survival in these churches is so low that the figures would tell us nothing, so all our information has to come from lost brasses. The picture is remarkably different from that of the counties. Brasses begin earlier (the result of very early local workshops in Lincoln and York), respect the 1340 depression, rise to a series of peaks in the fifteenth century, and fall off dramatically after 1480, the very time when brasses in parish churches were reaching their peak. They pay no attention to the mid-sixteenth-century troubles, and decline more or less steadily until the Civil War, when they virtually die out.

The differences are remarkable, and raise all sorts of questions. The reason for so low a survival rate compared with the counties (7.5 per cent against 61.5 per cent) is of course historical and largely due to the fact that cathedrals were in large towns where a ready market was available for scrap metal, and the very large collections of brasses offered a standing temptation. In parish churches collections of brasses were often too small for plundering to be really worth while, and in country districts it was always more difficult to dispose of the metal.

The major difference is that in cathedrals the bulk of pro-

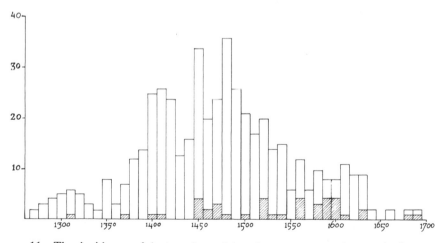

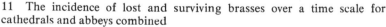

11 The incidence of lost and surviving brasses over a time scale for cathedrals and abbeys combined

duction comes earlier than in parish churches, and to a certain extent increasing numbers in cathedrals correspond to falling numbers in parish churches. One reason may be that in the fourteenth and fifteenth centuries wealth was still largely in the hands of the old nobility, who were supporters and benefactors of the churches, and many preferred to be buried not in their own parish churches but in the great cathedrals or abbeys, where they endowed chantries or obits. Also in the Middle Ages cathedrals and abbeys attracted a large entourage of minor officials and servants, and there are records of many brasses in cathedrals to such men—organists, choirmasters, master masons, carpenters, even a brass engraver. The cathedral staff proper was also large, secular cathedrals having a choir of vicars; and of course the monasteries flourished. All this began to change after the end of the Middle Ages in 1485. Vocations declined in monasteries and among cathedral staffs, and wealth was transferred into the hands of a new bourgeoisie. Current sceptical ideas weakened religion, and cathedral and abbey retainers fell away. On the whole it would appear that the newly enriched classes preferred to be commemorated in their own parish churches, where their tombs would be noticed by all their neighbours, rather than be lost in the vastness of a cathedral. Certainly it is noticeable that cathedral brasses drop off very steeply immediately after Bosworth Field, and the boom in prosperity of the reign of Henry VII had no effect on them.

Likewise the slump under Henry VIII made little impression, since the few who were still being buried in cathedrals, largely the clergy, were little affected by general economic trends. The second flowering under Elizabeth also had no effect on cathedrals, for it would appear that under the Tudors they ceased to play any significant part in the life of the nation and were left rather in a backwater. Monasteries, of course, except for those taken over as new cathedrals, were out of the running altogether. It is hardly surprising that the Civil War finished off cathedral brasses once and for all.

DISTRIBUTION BY TYPES

Turning away from the general picture of brasses, it is worth looking at their division by class or type, and at what proportions have been lost in different categories. Fig 12 shows each category of brass (the surviving items shaded) as a percentage of the total (above), for cathedrals and for parish churches, and also shows (below) what proportion (shaded) survives within each category. It will be noticed firstly that whereas in parish churches there are more figure brasses than inscriptions, in cathedrals it is the other way round, possibly because of the large number of fairly poor clerics or retainers commemorated on cathedral brasses. Survival rates for inscriptions and effigies in parish churches are by chance exactly equal, at 61.5 per cent. More effigies than inscriptions survive in cathedrals, but on the whole the number of surviving cathedral brasses is so small that it is unsafe to draw any general conclusion from them.

Of individual types it is not surprising that figures of ecclesiastics (surviving and lost) form by far the largest group in cathedrals, making 23 per cent of the total. Civilians and episcopal figures come a rather poor second, at 7 per cent, forty examples each. Only 5 per cent of brasses show wives on their husband's brasses, equal to the number of crosses. Other types are insignificant. (Looking at the plain inscriptions in more detail, where this is possible, one can see that a much higher proportion of laymen to ecclesiastics are commemorated by these plainer and cheaper monuments.)

In parish churches the largest category is double brasses of civilians and wives: 32 per cent of all brasses show civilian effigies, and 33 per cent show wives on their husbands' brasses (the discrepancy is due to wives on military or legal brasses). There are precisely half as many military effigies as civilians, a fact that will surprise many. Ecclesiastics come next, followed by brasses showing women alone and lawyers and academics, though most of the last are in Oxford. Other elements are not significant. Not surprisingly, episcopal brasses are rare in parish churches.

On the whole this is the sort of distribution we should expect-ecclesiastics dominating in cathedrals, and civilians and their wives in parish churches. In fact the addition of material from lost brasses makes very little difference to the proportions.

Examining what proportion of each category is lost, however, shows some anomalies (Fig 12, below). In cathedrals, civilians and military effigies have good survival rates (over 20

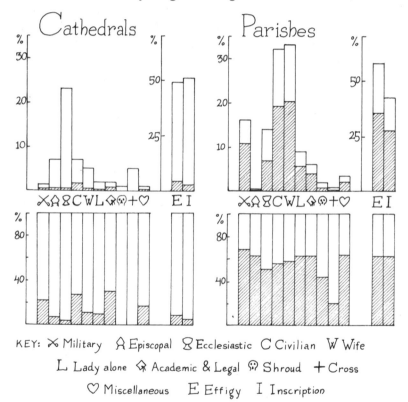

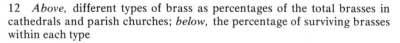

KEY: ✗ Military   ♙ Episcopal   ♟ Ecclesiastic   C Civilian   W Wife
L Lady alone   ♘ Academic   & Legal   ♟ Shroud   + Cross
♡ Miscellaneous   E Effigy   I Inscription

12 *Above,* different types of brass as percentages of the total brasses in cathedrals and parish churches; *below,* the percentage of surviving brasses within each type

per cent), and 30 per cent of legal and academic brasses survive. Most of these, however, are post-Reformation. Shroud and cross brasses have vanished altogether, and the survival rates of other categories only averages 10 per cent.

In parish churches the best rate of survival is among military brasses, at 68 per cent, possibly because local squires tended to keep a watchful eye on their ancestors' brasses, and even kept them in repair, as at Stopham. Ecclesiastics have a comparatively low rate of survival, only 50 per cent, perhaps because they had no descendants, and there may have been an undercurrent of feeling in the seventeenth and eighteenth centuries that Popish priests did not deserve much consideration. Cross brasses have suffered most severely, almost certainly because of their fragile nature and not deliberate destruction. None of those that survive are undamaged, and comparison of old rubbings and drawings shows that they tended to fall apart gradually. More surprising is the fact that shroud and skeleton brasses have suffered severely, only 43 per cent surviving in parish churches, and, as we have seen, none at all in cathedrals. There has always been a tendency to look on them with some disgust, and this may have encouraged their destruction—though they may also have appealed to the antiquity hunter as macabre and original souvenirs.

A rather surprising result of the tabulated figures is the high survival rate in general: the largest categories show a survival rate of 55 to 68 per cent, and the average of all brasses is just over 60 per cent. This percentage is a great contrast to the traditional estimate of 10 per cent. It is true that accounts of brasses are necessarily incomplete, but without evidence it would be rash to presume significantly large quantities lost without trace. On the whole, including cathedrals and monasteries, it might be fair to say that half the brasses have survived. This is the same proportion as was estimated by Haines, who very often is proved right against later authorities.

Looking at the different categories against a time scale,

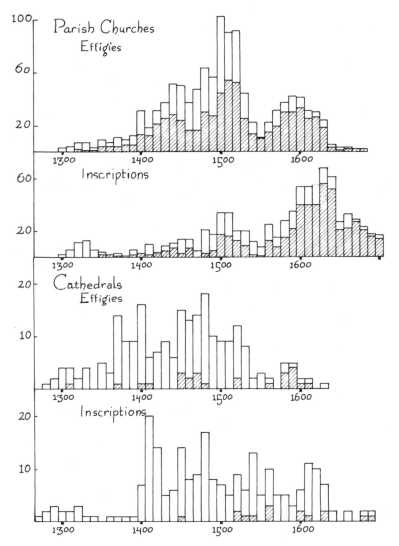

13　Brasses divided into effigies and inscriptions, against a time scale, for cathedrals and parish churches

various other facts appear. On a simple division into effigies and inscriptions (Fig 13) it becomes clear that the bulk of pre-Reformation brasses are effigies, the bulk of later ones inscriptions—a fact we could have deduced from surviving examples. An exception occurs in the earliest period, when a large number of plain inscriptions in separate letters were produced, of which only one mutilated example survives at Dean. After 1350 plain inscriptions rather went out of fashion in parish churches until the end of the sixteenth century, though in cathedrals they were common in the fifteenth.

After the Reformation, inscriptions become more widespread, perhaps partly because of religious sentiment against images, but more likely simply through economy or a desire to avoid ostentation. Many of these plain inscriptions are in fact to very wealthy and high ranking people, such as Archbishops of Canterbury at Lambeth and Oxford, earls at Petworth and Arundel, and the children of dukes at Lambeth. The post-Civil War revival is almost entirely composed of inscriptions, many of which are in fact coffin-plates set up on the walls as memorials. In cathedrals almost all post-Reformation brasses are inscriptions.

The great slump in the middle of the sixteenth century affected effigy brasses much more than it did inscriptions, since the total number of effigies in 1550 is only $10\frac{1}{2}$ per cent of the figure for 1500, while for inscriptions the percentage is $23\frac{1}{2}$. This is not very surprising in view of the fact that it was economic decline that caused the slump, and the cheaper type of brass might well have been expected to continue.

Looking at different categories of effigy brass over the date scale (Fig 14), we find that the largest categories, civilians and women, were late starters, but in general follow the pattern for brasses as a whole. It will be noticed that on surviving brasses alone there appear to be more civilian brasses in the Elizabethan period than before, and female brasses have approximately equal peaks in 1600 and 1500. The evidence from lost brasses, however, shows clearly that both categories

129

ran true to form, with a very much higher production in 1500.

Ecclesiastical brasses tend to fluctuate little throughout the fifteenth century, but fall off at the Reformation, though, unlike the normal pattern, their greatest decline comes about 1530, when the Reformation really began, not in 1520, like others. They never recover, and the loss of church revenues and the declining social position of the clergy is reflected in their brasses.

Military brasses exhibit the peculiarity of continuing with very little drop throughout the sixteenth century, only falling off finally at the beginning of the seventeenth. There is a peak in 1440, and a drop for the Wars of the Roses, which wiped out much of the medieval military class. Many of the new ruling class under Henry VII took over the positions of country squires, and liked to be shown in armour, though

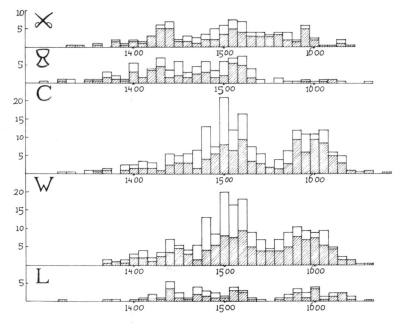

14   The principal types of brass against a time scale. For key to symbols, see Fig 12

probably many of them never wore it. (It is noticeable how the title 'Lord of the Manor' is more common on the brasses of new families, who felt the need to assert their new positions, than on those of the old, who could let it be taken for granted.) This new class of country squires managed to acquire a fair proportion of the old monastic wealth, with which they kept up their prosperity throughout the century; their brasses reflect this up to the accession of James I, when their numbers declined as militarism went out of fashion.

Other categories of brass are too small for them to be plotted with any real significance. Legal and academic brasses form a steady trickle from 1400 to the mid-seventeenth century, with a very small peak in 1500. Shroud and skeleton brasses have a short run from 1450 to 1530, and are most popular c1500, with the odd mid-seventeenth century example in a very different taste. Cross brasses as a category are known almost entirely from lost examples, and it is traditional to say that they come to an abrupt end at the Reformation. In fact they are common throughout the fourteenth century but become rare after c1420, and are very scarce indeed in the early sixteenth century. There are no known examples enclosing figures after 1420, and the later examples are plain or are crucifixes. (Both forms are in fact known on post-Reformation brasses, though by chance not in the areas under analysis.)

Miscellaneous brasses that refuse to fit into any real patterns include figures of saints in the Middle Ages, and allegorical compositions later on. The former were most popular around 1500 and the latter around 1600.

These figures and results are still to a large extent provisional. For the areas covered they probably represent a true picture, though in detail should not be relied on as absolutely accurate. It is often difficult to date an indent precisely, and though only those for which approximate dates can be provided have been included, there is room for considerable adjustment, especially in the early period. Moreover it is of course impossible to be certain that all documentary evidence for lost brasses is correct in giving the date, for errors of transcription by a seventeenth-century copyist may have mis-dated brasses by centuries. There is usually no way of telling whether a lost brass was laid down at the date given on the inscription, or many years before or after. Surviving examples are often found to be of earlier or later date than the date of death. With some we have evidence: we know that the seven brasses to Archbishops of York with dates from the eleventh and twelfth centuries were all laid by Archbishop Thoreson in 1368. But what are we to make of the six brasses in Lincoln claiming to be thirteenth-century? We know that brasses were produced in Lincoln from 1272 on, but two are recorded from 1253 and 1258.

In several instances the evidence from lost brasses makes a very significant difference in the pattern of distribution by date and type from that which could be obtained from surviving brasses alone. In other cases it makes little difference. Perhaps the most important new fact to have emerged is the upsurge of brasses about 1500, though other facts, such as the very different picture to be obtained from cathedral and abbey brasses, can also be deduced from a study of lost brasses alone. The results, based as they are on figures for only a small proportion of English brasses, can hardly yet be extrapolated into general conclusions, but they do at least prove that we cannot safely rely on evidence from surviving brasses alone.

DISTRIBUTION BY AREA

In Figs 15 and 16 respectively an attempt is made to plot the distribution of lost and surviving brasses in the two most coherent areas from which lost brasses have been recorded—Bedfordshire with Huntingdonshire, and Sussex with Surrey. Each circle represents a church containing brasses, the circles varying in size according to the total number of brasses

132

recorded, and the proportion surviving in each church being shown in black.

At first sight there seems to be very little pattern in the way in which brasses are distributed; they do not follow river valleys as such but are simply found in towns and villages that tend to follow river valleys or spring lines. Large collections of brasses do not always mean large towns: one of the largest collections in Sussex is at the tiny village of Stopham, while

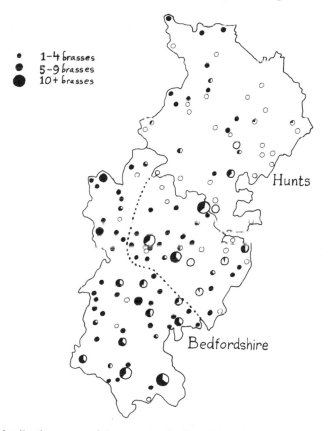

15 Distribution map of brasses in Bedfordshire and Huntingdonshire. Circles each represent one church and are blackened proportionately to the number of brasses surviving therein. Bedfordshire has been divided into plains and high ground

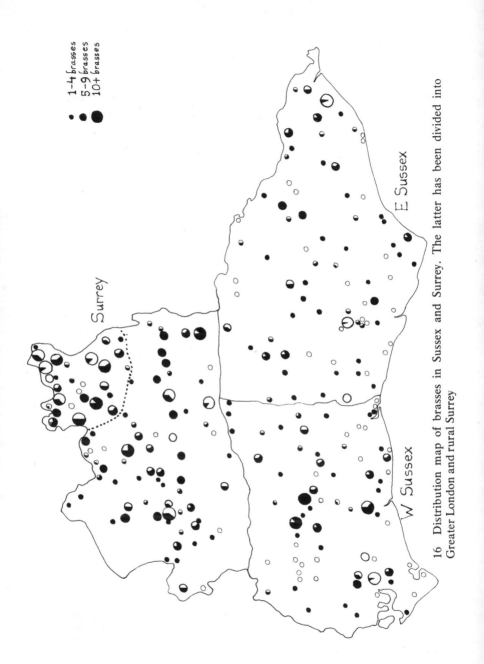

16 Distribution map of brasses in Sussex and Surrey. The latter has been divided into Greater London and rural Surrey

1-4 *brasses*
5-9 *brasses*
10+ *brasses*

Surrey

E Sussex

W Sussex

most of the important medieval towns, such as Steyning, Pevensey or Hastings, have hardly anything to show. However, it is noticeable that there is more of a concentration of brasses in Surrey than in any other county, becoming thicker towards London. This is only to be expected, considering not only that the wealth of London has always tended to spill over into Surrey but also that the majority of brasses were made in London, and would have been cheaper the shorter distance they had to travel. It is also noticeable that brasses in northern Bedfordshire and Huntingdonshire, the Fen country, are more scattered, and that a greater proportion are lost.

Putting this information into figures, we find that Surrey has a total of 518 brasses, whereas the whole of Sussex has only 454 in nearly three times the area. Bedfordshire and Huntingdonshire between them have only 358, in an area slightly smaller than Sussex.

The proportion of lost brasses is more revealing. In West Sussex, for example, 60 per cent of all brasses survive, a proportion very close to the general average. In East Sussex it is surprisingly high, at 76.5 per cent. Surrey taken as a whole has only 57 per cent surviving, but if we divide off the area closely under the influence of London and now governed by London (see dotted line, Fig 16), we find that only 42 per cent of brasses have survived, as against 63 per cent in the rest of Surrey. Similarly, if Bedfordshire is divided into the high ground or pastoral country in the south, and the flat lands merging with the Fens in the north (see dotted line, Fig 16), we find a survival rate of 77.5 per cent in the hills and only 48 per cent in the plain. Only 34.5 per cent of brasses survive in Huntingdonshire.

Looking closer, we find that the largest single collection in West Sussex was at Chichester, with forty-five brasses, all but five of them lost. Rural West Sussex has a survival rate of 71 per cent, closer to that for East Sussex. Again, if we were to abstract all market towns from Surrey, the rural areas would be found to have a much higher survival rate.

135

These statistics seem to lead to two widely different conclusions. In the south brasses were largely lost from towns or their environs, and survived better in rural areas; in the Midlands brasses survived in the hills, and suffered progressively more damage as the plains become fens.

The first conclusion is reasonable and has in fact long been a commonplace: that brasses survived more often in remote country churches than in towns has already been indicated by the very high losses shown from cathedrals. The main reason was probably the ready market for scrap metal provided in a town, for thieves or churchwardens could dispose of the brasses easily, and there would be enough to make it worth while. In the country often there was only a single brass in a church, and it would have been that much less attractive to tear it up and carry it all the way to the nearest town to dispose of the metal for perhaps only a few pence. Also town churches tended to be restored, pewed or refloored during the worst periods of the seventeenth and eighteenth centuries, when brasses were sold off without consideration. It is true that restorations did much damage in country churches, but they tended to survive unrestored till the nineteenth century, when at least some care was taken of brasses. Moreover many country churches were watched over by local squires who took some interest in their own family tombs, and the only church in all the counties surveyed where a group of over ten brasses (fourteen to be precise) has survived with no losses at all is Stopham, where the brasses were constantly maintained, small missing parts replaced and extra figures or shields added by the local family.

Why then is the situation so different in Bedfordshire and Huntingdonshire? The more remote the churches are the more the brasses seem to have been lost. It is at this point that we remember that Cromwell was born in Huntingdon, Bunyan in Bedford. In fact, as we have seen, there is no reliable evidence to connect the Puritans with the destruction of brasses, except for the activities of people like Dowsing, who removed only certain parts and not complete brasses; but it seems suspicious that there should have been such heavy losses in the very cradle of Puritanism, and one wonders whether perhaps there is some connection. If so, it is unlikely that it was due to official policy. Bunyan was not the sort of man to go around desecrating churches, however much he might disapprove of the doctrine preached in them (though, of course, he was a scrap metal dealer before his conversion!). On the whole devout Puritans would have avoided the established churches and worshipped in their own meeting houses. Perhaps the answer is simply that in areas with a nonconforming tradition the established churches were neglected and ill attended, and with few to watch over them or care for them they were vulnerable to thieving and speculation by churchwardens. The collective conscience of the neighbourhood would be much less liable to regard the old churches and their fittings with any awe or respect, and it may well be that general neglect and apathy produced the effect commonly attributed to fanaticism.

When Mr Page-Phillips published a distribution map of surviving pre-1700 brasses calculated by counties, Huntingdonshire stood out as an area with very few brasses surrounded by a much denser distribution.[2] Adding in the lost brasses would certainly remove the discrepancy, which brings us to the whole question of how a distribution map of the British Isles would be altered by a survey of all lost brasses.

The present distribution in England is thickest in the Thames valley and Norfolk, and thins out in concentric rings to the poorly endowed areas of Northumbria, Wales and Devon. Obviously it will take many years of further research, cataloguing indents and examining records, before a valid distribution map can be made for the whole country. It is a commonplace in archaeology that distribution maps tend to plot only the distribution of archaeologists.

Information so far on lost brasses is most complete in the Thames valley simply because there has been more work done here than elsewhere, with certain exceptions, notably the more spectacular sites such as York and Lincoln. Information from the north and west is still very inadequate. There are so far records of only two lost brasses from Cumberland, none from Westmorland, and two from Northumberland; and even Durham, with one of the finest cathedrals in England, can only muster twenty-one, hardly more than a tenth of the number at York. Hardly any losses are known from Lancashire, though perhaps an area that stubbornly remained Catholic after the Reformation preserved what few brasses it had. Again very little has been done on indents from Wales, Cornwall and Devon.

It may be that these statistics are representative, for there are very few surviving brasses in these areas, but it is too early to quote them as reliable. Scotland, an equally unpromising area, has been thoroughly investigated by Mr Greenhill, who has found twenty-seven indents and records of three or four more lost brasses where only five or six survive.[3] Most of these were in the Lowlands, though there is an indent at Inverness and a rumour of a lost brass on Orkney. All these indents are of Tournai marble, showing that medieval Scots brasses were exclusively imported from the Continent, not from England. If this much information can be gathered from a thorough investigation of Scotland, it is probable that as much could be discovered about other areas with very few brasses.

On the whole it seems likely that the present pattern of distribution, centred on London, would be borne out by a thorough survey of lost brasses. Anomalies in the present distribution map are the very low numbers in Huntingdonshire and Leicestershire. As we have seen, Huntingdonshire's losses can be explained, and it is possible that Leicestershire too may have had an abnormally large proportion of lost brasses.

Possibly, if the figures for the whole of Lincolnshire were known, it would come much higher on the list, joining with

Norfolk to form a second centre round the Wash. Lincoln had a very early local workshop, all but one of whose products are lost, while Norwich had a later workshop whose products are largely responsible for the great number of brasses surviving there—and imported brasses from Flanders through the Wash ports and the Humber.

Areas that certainly need more investigation are the Channel Islands and Ireland. No brasses at all survive in the Channel Islands, though there are reports of several indents on Guernsey. The medieval churches of Ireland have suffered so much that it is hardly surprising that only six brasses survive in the whole country, though there must have been many more.

SUMMARY

This chapter has been more in the nature of experiment and inquiry than of final conclusions. The sample analysed is only about a tenth of the material in the British Isles, so that, although the conclusions reached have a good chance of being valid, they may be totally belied by further research. What is certain is that we cannot draw valid conclusions from surviving brasses alone, since losses, though in all probably only half or less of the total, are not random but apparently selective, both in terms of the dates of the brasses lost and the areas.

In order to produce really useful results it would be necessary to have documentary and archaeological research carried out over at least half the British Isles, including a fair proportion of counties or areas very poorly supplied with brasses. The documentary work should not impose any great obstacles, since the bulk of the material is likely to be available in a few good libraries. The field work, however, would be a major undertaking, for while it proved possible for an energetic cyclist to survey all the churches of West Sussex, it would be a very different proposition to cover the whole of

Yorkshire. The work currently undertaken by the Monumental Brass Society relies on a large number of field workers each entrusted with a relatively small area, and there is a reasonable chance that the indents at least of England will have been listed by the end of the century.

Once the material is collected, there will be many further fields for analysis and study in greater detail, such as investigation of social groupings represented by brasses; more detailed analysis by types, going into such details as whether they are canopied or not, and distinguishing between large and elaborate brasses and small cheap ones; and the study of type distribution by area or by date. To a certain extent the study of styles and workshops can be helped by lost brasses, though normally it is impossible to distinguish the style of a brass from indents or documentary sources. Some local workshops may leave very distinct indents, as Mr Greenwood has shown in his analysis of the Bedford-Cambridge workshop,[4] and the early Lincolnshire workshop identified by Mr Blair is known almost entirely from the indents for separate-letter inscriptions. Occasionally, too, an old drawing or rubbing may identify lost brasses from one of the London workshops (see Fig 7 and Plate 1b), though one cannot always trust old drawings to show the details accurately enough. Flemish imports, of course, can easily be distinguished by their use of Tournai marble for the indents, by references in the antiquaries to 'stones plated all over' and the like. The field is open for further research, which it is to be hoped will be carried out with useful and reliable results.

Notes for this chapter appear on page 188

6

ASPECTS OF BRASSES

It is to empty slabs again that one has to look for types of brass of which no complete exampes have come down to us . . . (Mill Stephenson)

There would be no point in studying lost brasses and collecting information about them if it did not help us to understand and appreciate those that remain. A mere list is of little value, but if we combine our knowledge of lost brasses with that of surviving ones, we can draw some new conclusions, provide parallels for unique examples, fill gaps in otherwise perplexing sequences, and investigate categories now totally unrepresented. In this chapter a number of aspects of the study of brasses are examined in the light of lost examples on which we have found information, in an attempt to show what a significant difference the added information can make.

BRASSES BEFORE THE BLACK DEATH

The origin of brasses is still a subject needing extensive research and study. Their relationship to incised slabs and Limoges enamels has long been taken for granted, though in fact there may well be two distinct remote sources—the simple coffin lid with an embossed cross, and the three-dimensional effigy. It is clear, however, that brasses as we know them evolved in France, and were perfected in the workshops of St

141

Denis before the middle of the thirteenth century.[1] The drawings of Roger de Gaignières show some 3,500 French incised slabs and brasses, including many brasses dating from the thirteenth century. The earliest monument that is certainly a true brass and not an incised slab is dated to 1241, at Sens, though others of earlier date may well have been of brass.[2] There is a clear development from this early French school to the fourteenth century Flemish and English schools, which use many of the same basic ideas though in original ways. From the Flemish in turn derived the first regular German workshops in the fifteenth century. A few French brasses were exported and also copied locally, and the famous series of early Silesian brasses seem to be derived from St Denis models.[3] From these and the de Gaignières drawings it seems clear that the French used inscriptions of separate Lombardic letters, so it was possibly French craftsmen who laid the first such brass inscription in England, in the mosaic paving in front of the high altar of Westminster Abbey in 1268. The floor itself was made by Odoric of Rome, but there is no parallel for the brass inscription on Roman work, and he must have collaborated with French or English craftsmen.[4]

French brasses were commonly enamelled, and there are two surviving examples in St Denis to the royal children Jean and Blanche, which are transitional between the Limoges enamel and the true brass (enamelled plates, of course, have to be of pure copper, not brass). A similar tomb was made for Walter de Merton, Bishop of Rochester, in 1277: records at Merton College include the payment of £11 5s 6d 'liberat' Magistro Johanni Burgensi Limovicensis pro tumba dict' Episcopi Roffensis scilicet pro construccione et cariagio de Lymoges usque Roffam.' This was set in £22 worth of carved stonework, 'mazeoneria circa dictam tumbam defuncti', which was brought from London.[5]

There are many brasses, indents or rumours of them in England which are commonly placed in the thirteenth century, sometimes even in the first half of that century. The most famous is the 'founder's brass' in St Paul's, Bedford, to Simon do Beauchamp, who died in 1208, though it is now generally agreed that the brass in question was laid some 150 years later. Other such 'early brasses' are the result of the wrong attribution of surviving indents, such as 'Bishop Bingham, 1247' at Salisbury, which is a mis-attribution of the indent for Bishop Mortival, 1330, or, like that at Bedford, they are genuine brasses laid long after the date of death. None of the spectacular early brasses can be authenticated, and it is remarkable that despite the southern origin of brasses there does not seem to have been a regular workshop in the south until the fourteenth century. Two isolated fragments in Westminster Abbey dating from 1276 and 1277 may have been produced by an early London workshop, but they have no parallels save a few loose letters.[6] The first genuine workshop seems to have been, oddly enough, in the remote county of Lincolnshire, and the first accurately dated brass was a very simple inscription in separate Lombardic letters to Dean William de Lexington, 1272, in Lincoln Minster. A few minute brass stops survive in the slab, as in the similar one to Archdeacon Simon de Barton, 1280. The lettering on these slabs is distinctive, and John Blair has identified a group of indents with similar lettering, all in or near Lincolnshire.[7] In Lincoln there were brasses of 1280 to Bishop Gravesend, which probably included a figure, and of 1288 to Anthony de Sarthorpe, both of which probably dated genuinely from the dates given, though the inscription to Bishop Grosteste, 1253, must have been laid some time after his death.

The inscription to Simon de Barton, and one at Navenby to Richard de Lue, before 1302, are on shaped stones that may have formed the lower halves of elongated quatrefoils, under half-effigies in relief. The Navenby slab marks the transition between two phases of Lincolnshire lettering. In the second phase there were several fine figure brasses, such as the knight on a bracket Sir Henry de Bayous (living in 1328, dead by 1336) at Linwood (Fig 17) and a priest, Robert de

143

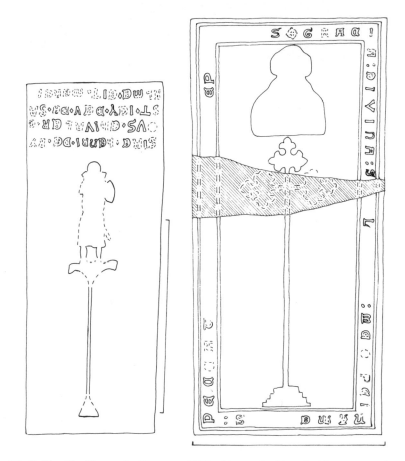

17 (*left*)   Sir Henry de Bayous, 1336, Linwood, Lincolnshire - an early knight on a bracket, of the Lincolnshire school
18 (*right*)   William de Meopham, 1322, Cranbrook, Kent - a typical cross brass with bust and separate-letter inscription

Clyderhow, 1334, at Sawley Abbey, Yorkshire. There are others that cannot yet be attributed to this group with certainty, while many more must be still undiscovered. The only surviving brass of the Lincolnshire school is the well-known one to Richard de Buslingthorpe (died after 1361, brass engraved c1330) at Buslingthorpe. The nearby tomb of his father (dead by 1345) shows an inscription with some characteristics of

Lincolnshire lettering, though the letter forms are normal 'main group' style, implying that the workshop ceased to function about that time, or at least ceased to use its own distinctive lettering.

There is some evidence that there may have been a similar workshop operating at the end of the thirteenth century in Yorkshire, and it is possible that there were others not yet identified. The main London workshops do not seem to have started until the beginning of the fourteenth century, and did not gain control of the market until nearly half way through it. The earliest datable 'main group' brass was that of Bishop William de Luda, 1299, in Ely Cathedral, whose indent shows a figure under a canopy with an inscription in separate letters. From then until about 1360 a very large number of brasses were produced with this sort of lettering, which John Blair has shown was produced in standard forms and three standard sizes, found all over the country. The letters were cast, not cut out, so the forms are uniform. Several of these inscriptions include the date: for instance, Martin Hampton, 1306, at Ickham, Kent; Richard Oliver, 1327, at Great Horkesley, Essex; and Reynald Alard, 1354, at Winchelsea, Sussex. These three dates seem to indicate the time span during which very similar brasses were produced. Since the majority are undated, however, and cannot be dated by documentary evidence, the date sequence for this period remains very vague.

Many of these brasses are simply inscriptions, either in lines across the slab (St Mary the Virgin, Oxford) or around the edges (St Paul's, Bedford; White Waltham, Berkshire; Jesus College, Cambridge; Hornchurch, Essex; Hunstanton, Norfolk; Peterborough Cathedral; Elsfield, Oxfordshire; Stoke by Nayland, Suffolk; or Albury, Surrey). Others surround incised or embossed crosses, as at Christchurch in Oxford, East Lavant in Sussex and Tewkesbury in Gloucestershire, the last a very fine example with riveted letters that is datable to 1347. Some enclose incised figures, forming in fact part of monuments that are classified as incised slabs, not

145

brasses, as at Pyrton, Oxfordshire, and Elsing, Norfolk.

Probably the commonest type among all these early brasses is the separate letter inscription enclosing a brass cross, either plain, flory or crocketed (Cockayne Hatley, Bedfordshire; Harwell, Berkshire; Rampton, Cambridgeshire; Tilty, Essex; St Neot's, Huntingdonshire; Reculver, Kent; Pulham, Norfolk; Brixworth, Northamptonshire; Christ Church, Oxford; Carlton, Suffolk; Great Bedwyn, Wiltshire; or Skirlaw, Yorkshire). Others show a half-effigy above the cross (Cranbrook, Kent [Fig 18]; Hornchurch, Essex; Christchurch, Hampshire; Garsington, Oxfordshire; Buxted, Sussex; or Ramsbury, Wiltshire). Sometimes this half-effigy is canopied, as on the slab of Prior Norton in St Alban's; at other times the cross itself is canopied, as at Askerswell and Whitchurch Canonicorum, Dorset (two parts of the same slab). Others show half, three-quarter or even full-length figures in the head of a foliated cross, as at St Mary the Virgin, Oxford, though this form did not become popular until the second half of the fourteenth century.

In addition to all these crosses there were many full-length life-size figures, often under canopies with various accessories. There are examples with separate-letter inscriptions at Bottisham, Cambridgeshire; Hever, Kent; Stoke by Nayland, Suffolk; and Laycock Abbey, Wiltshire; and fragments from Llanfaes Priory, Anglesey; Dunwich, Suffolk; and Hardwick Mill, Oxfordshire (from Eynsham Abbey).

It is worth noting that, although the fillet inscription was to supersede the separate-letter inscription, they did co-exist, and fillets may be as early as, or earlier than, separate letters. A large number of cross brasses have distinctive little animals at the foot of the cross, and these are so similar that obviously they were cut from the same stencil (Fig 19). Most of these brasses have separate-letter inscriptions (Watlington, Norfolk; Christ Church, Oxford or Hartley, Kent), but some have fillets (Great Hale, Lincolnshire; and St Alban's). Three brasses show curious devices powdering the slab (Fig 28);

those at Trotton, Sussex, and in St Paul's Cathedral had separate-letter inscriptions, and that at Saltwood, Kent, had a fillet.

Besides the common and widely distributed products of the main workshops, there seems to have been a small and exclusive workshop producing immense and very elaborate brasses, with life-size figures, generally on little brackets, and large canopies with saints, angels and heraldry, usually within fillet inscriptions, though some have separate letters. The largest examples are those of Bishop Haselshaw of Wells, 1308, and Bishop Beaumont of Durham, 1333, but others, such as Maud de Burgh at Tewkesbury, 1315, and Abbot Wallingford of St Albans, 1335, are only slightly smaller. The mutilated

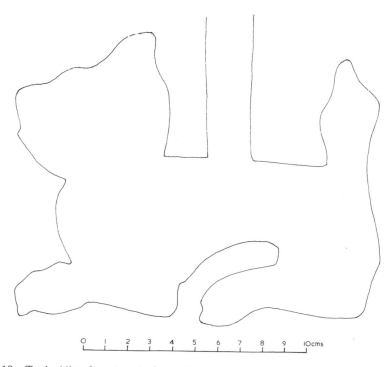

19   Typical lion found at the foot of the cross on many early slabs

figure of Archbishop Greenfield at York may be the only sur-
vivor from this group.

Nearly all these early brasses are lost. Of the separate-letter
inscriptions, only that to Walter de Ireland, 1311, at Dean,
Bedfordshire, survives, and that through the accident of
having been walled up for centuries. Four crosses remain but
all are severely mutilated. Hardly a dozen figures and a few
half-effigies and fragments survive of all the pre-Black Death
brasses; they are impressive enough, but not representative of
what has been lost. Without a study of lost brasses, indeed,
the few survivors are almost meaningless, and many misconceptions have arisen as a result of looking at them in isolation.
In particular they have been inaccurately dated, and even the
sequence of the development of armour has been confused as
a result. Claude Blair, Mr Page-Phillips and others have
shown that all the surviving mail-clad knights belong to the
period 1320-40,[8] and that there is probably no real difference
in date between the plain mail depicted on the Acton or
Trumpington brasses and the mail partly reinforced with
plate or boiled leather at Pebmarsh and Gorleston. Since
there are so many more lost brasses than survivors, it is not
surprising that many of the former can be dated more
accurately than the latter; in fact a date sequence could be
constructed from lost brasses that would be impossible from
survivors, and surviving figures can be redated by reference to
lost but well-dated brasses. For example, the brass of Sir
Richard de Buslingthorpe is traditionally dated from 1290 to
1310, and enjoyed a short reign as 'the earliest brass in England' after the redating of the large knights. John Blair,
however, has shown that it has an inscription in a developed
form of the second phase of Lincolnshire lettering, and therefore cannot be much earlier than 1330.

CROSSES AND RELIGIOUS EMBLEMS

It has customarily been imagined that crosses and all other

religious devices on brasses were particularly singled out for destruction by fanatics, and for that reason few survive. To a certain extent this seems to be true of explicit religious scenes or images, and we have seen that William Dowsing did remove a Virgin and Child at Cambridge, though he left a Trinity at Orford. Nowhere, however, does his diary or his commission mention crosses other than crucifixes, and there is no evidence whatsoever that plain crosses or those that had figures only of the deceased were ever destroyed as a policy. They were lost simply because of their fragility.

Throughout the fourteenth century crosses were the most common type of brass, and they remained popular until about 1420. Before the development of brasses, crosses were the most common type of marking on gravestones, either carved in relief or incised into flat surfaces. Many thousands of these cross slabs survive from the twelfth, thirteenth and fourteenth centuries, and we can see in them many parallels to the forms taken by cross brasses.

It became the fashion in the thirteenth century to carve stone coffin-lids as if they had openings-either a trefoil-shaped opening revealing the head and shoulders of the deceased, with the cross lying further down on the breast, or an opening in the centre of the cross itself revealing just the head, or occasionally, lower down, revealing just the hands holding a heart. Often another opening at the bottom showed the tips of the shoes. The 'bodies' thus partly revealed were always shown alive and clothed, unlike the cadavers of a later period.

These carved openings must have formed very inconvenient irregularities in the paving of churches, and so the same effect was transferred to two-dimensional incised slabs and brasses. Thus developed the two most common ways of showing an effigy with a cross: a half-effigy or bust above a plain cross, or a head in the centre of the cross which gradually developed into a full-length effigy.

The plain cross remained the most popular. Examples have already been quoted from the early period, but later plain crosses have been lost, for instance, from Sithney, Cornwall; Danbury, Terling and Tolleshunt d'Arcy, Essex; Winchester Cathedral; Dorchester and Launton, Oxfordshire; Mickleham, Surrey; Hooe, Sussex; Wells Cathedral; Aldborough, Yorkshire; and York Minster. Many of these, although classified as 'plain' by virtue of having no human figure, were in fact quite elaborate: most had floriated arms, many had animals at the base (at Tilty, Essex, an elephant), some were crocketed, others, as at Aldborough, had branches down the stem from which shields were suspended, and a few had canopies. Plain crosses in fact survived the general decline in cross brasses, and there were a few produced as late as the mid-sixteenth century, as at Singleton, Sussex.

Of figured crosses, the type showing half-effigies above the cross was virtually confined to the period before the Black Death, and a list of these has already been given. The second type, showing the figure in the cross head, came to supersede them, but early examples are difficult to detect from indents, since only a head was shown, and the whole outline was not much broader than that of a plain cross. Indents such as those at Little Easton and Great Horkesley, Essex, may have contained crosses closely resembling the surviving one at Chinnor, Oxfordshire. They become more obvious when the cross head opens out into a cusped quatrefoil or octofoil, and the head or half-effigy is separately inlaid in the middle; examples at Felsted, Essex, and St Mary the Virgin, Oxford, date from the early period. Some examples show pairs of half-effigies, though to begin with it was more normal to show two crosses. An unusual slab at Bepton, Sussex, has an incised cross between the indents for two brass half-effigies (Fig 20).

The old convention of showing the body through holes in the slab was soon forgotten, and by 1350 full-length effigies are appearing in cross heads. These remain popular until the early fifteenth century, and indents can be seen at Exeter Cathedral; Tormarton, Gloucestershire; Gillingham, Kent; and Merton College, Christ Church and St Mary the Virgin,

Oxford. At Great Doddington, Northamptonshire, the missing cross and figure have been skilfully restored by the vicar. Several crosses enclose double effigies of husband and wife. They were usually surrounded by marginal inscriptions, and were often accompanied by shields. One at Merton was flank-

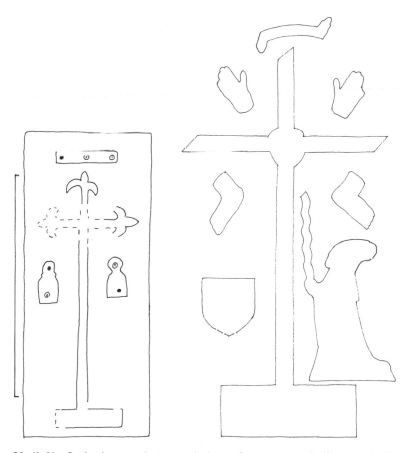

20 (*left*) Incised cross between indents for brass half-effigies, c1380, Bepton, Sussex

21 (*right*) Bishop John Underwood, 1541, St Andrew's, Norwich. The hands and feet, and the heart at the centre of the cross, symbolise the Five Wounds of Christ. The shield and top scroll survive

ed by two angels with scrolls, and had the Agnus Dei at the foot of the cross.

It is surprising how rarely crosses are depicted on brasses as objects of veneration, either with kneeling figures or with saints in the cross head. Where a saint is shown, it is usually the Virgin Mary, but they are extremely rare in cross heads. There is a simple example at Robertsbridge Abbey, Sussex. More elaborate, and forming a distinct though small subgroup, are those in which the figure kneels under an arch supporting the cross, and the Virgin is enthroned in its head. The prototypes are at Wotton under Edge, Gloucestershire, and the well-preserved indent of Adam de Brome, 1332, in St Mary's, Oxford. There are four similar indents in Ely Cathedral. A few plain crosses have kneeling figures at the foot, as shown by indents at Farnham, Surrey; Hanbury, Staffordshire; and St Alban's Abbey.

A rare variant of cross brass shows the Five Wounds of Christ, though when they are engraved on the cross itself (as on a palimpsest example at Hever, Kent), they do not, of course, show on indents. But one indent in St Andrew's, Norwich, clearly shows the Cross with the Heart in the centre and the hands and feet radiating from it. A figure of Bishop Underwood of Chalcedon, 1541, kneels at the base (Fig 21).[9]

Other odd cross brasses include a very small cross on an orb surrounded by a circular fillet inscription, at East Harling, Norfolk, and a Maltese cross with a half-effigy of a priest at St John's, Bedford. Two similar examples at St Paul's, Bedford, and Bolnhurst have plain Latin crosses standing on tall oblong bases that may have contained figures. A remarkable indent at Tolleshunt d'Arcy, Essex, shows a plain cross around whose head ran a circular inscription in separate letters, now unfortunately illegible.

Connected with cross brasses, though very different in purpose, are brass dedication crosses. Every church on consecration is marked with twelve crosses, and these are usually perpetuated in fresco or carving, but at Uffington, Berkshire, and Edington, Wiltshire, the indents remain for brass crosses surrounded by circles.

Artistically very similar to crosses are the curious phen omena of brackets. It is possible that these are vestigial cross

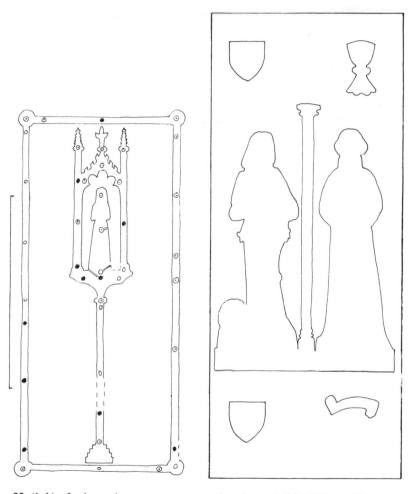

22 (*left*)   Lady under a canopy on a bracket, c1400, Higham Ferrers, Northamptonshire. A typical bracket brass
23 (*right*)   A man in armour and a priest in academics, with a pillar between them, c1490. An inexplicable arrangement, Pleshey, Essex.

153

stems, the figures having as it were outgrown the heads, but it is more likely that they derive from image brackets or pedestals. Several early indents, such as those of the great bishops at Durham and Wells, show the figures balancing on very small brackets. At Linwood, however, the bracket is twice as long as the figure, and the proportions range widely on later examples. Indents may be found at St Lawrence, Reading; Naseby, Northamptonshire; and Woodbridge, Suffolk. Like crosses, brackets are very fragile, and the few survivors are all damaged. They are often obviously designed from the same drawings: at Merton, for example, the surviving bracket brass to John Bloxham and John Whitton, which is undated, and the lost cross brass to Thomas Dolling, 1420, are so similar, with identical bases, they they must have been made at the

24   A civilian and wife kneeling to a tree, on which there may have been a crucifix, c1450, Waltham Abbey, Essex

same time and in the same workshop. Many brackets were surmounted by canopies, as on indents at Birdbrook and Saffron Walden, Essex; Reculver and Rolvenden, Kent; Higham Ferrers, Northamptonshire (Fig 22); and Catfield, Norfolk. At Clifton Campden, Staffordshire, the canopy encloses the whole bracket, stem and all.

It is much more common on brackets than crosses to find saints or the Trinity at the top, and the deceased kneeling below. The Blessed Virgin appears on canopied brackets at Burford, Oxfordshire; Hendon, Middlesex; Croydon, Surrey; and Lincoln Minster. At Sapcoate, Leicestershire, a curious indent shows a square tabernacle, which may have enclosed a Trinity, at the top of a long bracket stem. At Pleshey, Essex, another odd indent shows a pillar standing between the two figures, resembling the stem of a bracket or cross, but with nothing at the top (Fig 23).

A small and curious group of brasses that also seem to have affinities with crosses are tree brasses, where the major part of the design was a tree. One survives at St John Maddermarket, Norwich, but at least two very much more interesting ones are lost. An indent at Waltham Abbey, Essex, shows two kneeling figures under a large tree from which appears a scroll (Fig 24), and it would seem likely that a crucifix was depicted on the tree, as in a remarkable fifteenth-century painting entitled 'The Mystery of the Fall and Redemption of Man' by Giovanni da Moderna, and that the scroll was addressed to Christ or contained words spoken by him.[10]

Another remarkable tree brass from St Nicholas, King's Lynn, is preserved in a drawing of 1738 (Fig 25). It shows a flourishing tree, round which are tied two hearts on long strings, with the text *Ubi vera sunt gaudia, ibi nostra fixa sunt corda* (Where true joys are, there our hearts are fixed). Presumably again the tree stands for the cross, to which the hearts of believers are fixed. It commemorated Thomas Waterdeyn, c1415, Mayor of Lynn, and his wife Alice. Another possible tree brass, at Bray, Berkshire, is mentioned

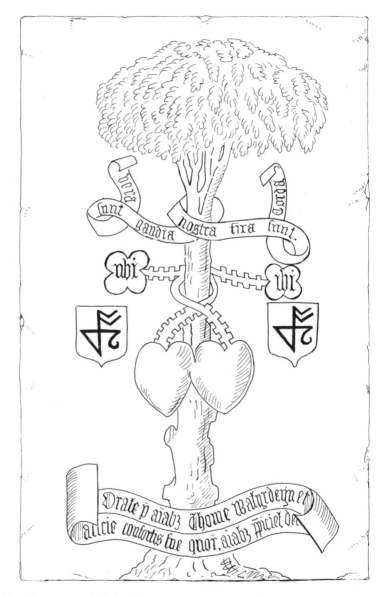

25 Thomas and Alice Waterdeyn, c1415, St Nicholas', King's Lynn, Norfolk. A very curious Heart brass, with a tree possibly symbolising the Cross. From a drawing by Mackerell

by Ashmole, who says that the brass of Thomas Foxley, 1426, had 'his feet resting upon a Tree', though here he may mean a bracket like that on the earlier Foxley brass

Christ crucified is an intrinsic part of the design of the Holy Trinity, which is common on surviving brasses, but crucifixes alone are known from many fewer examples. Fragments survive at Chelsfield, Kent, including most of the figure of Our Lady, who, with St John, appears regularly on crucifixes in painting and sculpture. At St Alban's they stand on the arms of the cross. In other surviving indents at Deddington, Oxfordshire, Lincoln and Worcester Cathedrals (two each), and at Monckton, Pembrokeshire, they do not appear, but the crucifix is distinctive in outline alone. At Connington, Huntingdonshire, it forms the central shaft of a double canopy, under which are two kneeling figures. On the whole, crucifixes seem to be later than plain crosses, and dated examples mostly come from the late fifteenth century or early sixteenth.

Scenes of the Resurrection and other aspects of the life of Christ date from about the same period. The Resurrection is sufficiently represented on surviving brasses, though Christ of the Apocalypse, seated on the rainbow (Revelation, 4,3) is only found on one surviving brass, at Sibstone, Leicestershire. Formerly there was a much more elaborate example on the back of a palimpsest at Shorne, Kent, showing the two-edged sword coming out of Christ's mouth, and the background powdered with stars.

William Dowsing tells us there was at Glensford, Suffolk, 'the Holy Ghost in brass', and if he is right, the representation of the Holy Ghost apart from its appearance in Trinities is unique. Another rarity was the Sacred Heart, inscribed *ihs* and surrounded by a crown of thorns, which was found in 1832 in St Dunstan in the West and subsequently lost, though an impression survives in the collection of the Society of Antiquaries.

The Blessed Virgin Mary was more common on brasses,

157

most frequently holding the Infant Christ, and several good representations survive. Lost examples have already been mentioned in the context of brackets and crosses. At St Benet's, Cambridge, she was shown in an oval frame or mandorla, and similar shapes on indents may have been the same. There used to be an example in the Austin Friary, London, but one at Dorchester, Oxfordshire, is less clear.

The Annunciation was surprisingly popular on brasses, as

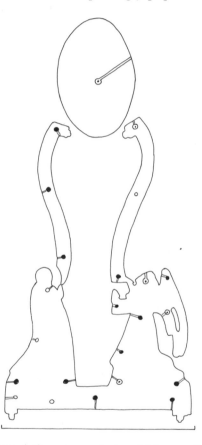

26   Either an Annunciation, or a priest and his guardian angel, c1450, Dorchester, Oxfordshire. The mandorla above may have enclosed God the Father or the Virgin Mary

in all branches of medieval art. Sometimes the scene was shown in a tabernacle or on a rectangular plate, leaving no distinctive indent, as in St Paul's on two brasses, but frequently the component parts-Gabriel, the Virgin, the lilypot and often the Hand of God above-were separately inlaid and left clear indents, as in York, Wells, Rochester and Ely Cathedrals; St Alban's and Tewkesbury Abbeys; Maidstone, Kent; St Margaret's, Westminster (Fig 4); and Ramsbury, Wiltshire. A very curious indent at Dorchester, Oxfordshire, shows a large kneeling figure, clearly an angel, facing another which is presumably either the Virgin, making this an exceptionally large Annunciation, or the deceased—in which case the Virgin was probably in the mandorla above (Fig 26). The Coronation of the Virgin was less popular in England, but is shown on indents at Cranbrook, Kent, and probably at Emneth, Norfolk.[11]

Other saints were frequently represented in the shafts of canopies and on the orphreys of copes. Many good examples survive, but it is clear that many more have gone. Such elaborate brasses were most common in cathedrals and monastery churches, which as we have seen, suffered from the greatest destruction of brasses. There were five such brasses in Durham, and four in St Paul's. Large individual figures of saints appeared on a few brasses, such as two at Lincoln to rectors of St Mary Magdalen's church, where the image of their patron saint formed the principal feature of each brass.

Figures of angels were formerly very common on canopies, on either side of the main pediment. They appear with censers at Horsheath, Cambridgeshire; Saltwood, Kent; Burton Agnes, Yorkshire; Tewkesbury, Gloucestershire; and Weekley, Northamptonshire. And they are standing on the pinnacles of the canopy at Wisbech, Cambridgeshire; Hawkesbury Upton, Gloucestershire; Canterbury Cathedral; and again at Saltwood. In the latter position they are often six-winged seraphim.

Elaborate composite religious scenes came usually fairly

late and were engraved on rectangular plates, so there is no evidence from indents. A rubbing survives of the one at St Mary Magdalen's, Oxford, where the people commemorated are shown being presented to the Trinity by their patrons (frontispiece). Although these religious scenes and figures are primarily associated with Catholic brasses, they did not die out completely at the Reformation, since angels and *putti* are comparatively common on seventeenth- and eighteenth-century brasses, and there is a figure of St George on a brass at Brentwood, Essex, dated 1672.

RANKS AND PROFESSIONS

Many trades, professions, social classes and dignities were formerly represented on brasses, of which few or none survive. This loss is greatest among the higher clergy, for reasons already stated. No brasses survive in England to cardinals though two fine ones are known to have been lost. One was to Cardinal Morton, in the Martyrdom at Canterbury, showing the cardinal's hat, and the other was at Lincoln to the Cardinal Bishop Philip de Ripingdon, 1424. A third at York to the Cardinal Archbishop Thomas Scot, 1480, apparently had no figure but only a pattern of scrolls.

Archbishops were best represented at York, where there were seven full-length figures, two half-effigies and three inscriptions to Archbishops of York. Seven of these were all laid at the same time by Archbishop Thoreson in 1368, but to judge by Torre's sketches of the indents, they were all highly individual and by no means a set of identical figures.[12] Archbishops of Canterbury were less often buried in their own cathedral and apparently less fond of brasses. There are only two indents of archbishops at Canterbury, though a third lies not far away at Maidstone. St Andrew's in Fife had two fine Flemish brasses to Archbishops James Stuart and William Scheres.

Bishops' brasses were extremely common, and many indents survive. There were nine at Lincoln, eight each at Chichester and Ely, seven at Durham and Worcester, four at Rochester, Norwich, and Lichfield, three at Winchester, Canterbury, Wells, Salisbury and Hereford, two at Exeter, York and St Paul's, and one each at Bangor, Orkney and Dunkeld. In addition simple inscriptions commemorated three more at Bangor and St Paul's, two more at Chester and another at Lincoln. Bishops were buried in parish churches at Haddenham, Cambridgeshire; Holbeach, Lincolnshire; St Andrew's, Norwich; Exton and Braunston, Rutland; Sudbury, Suffolk; Snaith and Sandford Parva, Yorkshire; and Tenby, Pem-

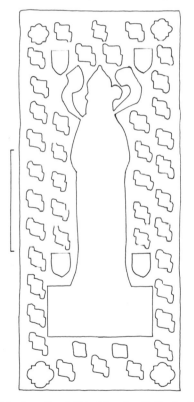

27 Bishop John Chedworth, 1471, Lincoln Cathedral. The bishop holds two large scrolls and the slab is powdered with scrolls

161

brokeshire. (Some of the mitred indents in Canterbury, Winchester, Ely, Durham and Worcester are probably to priors, not bishops, since in these great monastic cathedrals, where the bishop took the place of the abbot, the priors had complete jurisdiction over the monasteries and were granted the privilege of the mitre and pontificalia.)

This great range of episcopal brasses included many fine canopies with saints and other decorations, and probably comprised by far the richest class of brasses that ever existed. Certainly there is no surviving brass to match the size of the indent of Bishop Beaumont of Durham. A few old sketches of lost episcopal brasses show that many of them were larger and more magnificent than any surviving brass to a bishop; they were not all stereotyped in design, for variations in posture are found, some of the figures holding books or scrolls (Fig 27).

Brasses to mitred abbots are, of course, likely to be confused with those of bishops, and often identification of the rank commemorated on a mitred indent is a matter of guesswork. Mitred abbots were to be found on brasses in the abbeys of Gloucester and Westminster (three each), Peterborough (two, though one did not show the mitre), Bayham, Fountains and St Alban's (five). At Fountains the mitre was not on but above the head, possibly implying that its possessor died before he could be blessed as abbot. The indents in St Alban's are the most splendid, as befitted one of the richest houses in Europe. Other abbots are buried in country churches belonging to their abbeys, to which they may have retired, as at Wrestlingworth, Bedfordshire; Hawkesbury Upton, Gloucestershire; and Nether Wallop, Hampshire. There is said to have been one in the parish church at Battle, wearing vestments and a 'military hat', and there is an indent probably to another abbot of Battle in a kitchen garden at Priesthawes, East Sussex.[13]

Unmitred abbots holding croziers are shown on indents at Bindon and Milton Abbeys, Dorset; Byland Abbey, Yorkshire; Queen Charlton, Somerset; and Newton by Folkingham, Lincolnshire. At Saffron Walden, Essex, Abbot Price of Conway, 1528, was shown in cope with crozier. Some of these indents have only been discovered by excavation, and it is possible that more may yet be found. Recently a fragmentary indent for an abbot of Eynsham was found at Hardwick Mill, Oxfordshire.[14] Brasses of abbots were often simpler than those of bishops, many consisting just of a simple figure and inscription. The two in Dorset were like this, and very early.

Many abbots and a few bishops were commemorated not by figures but by croziers alone. Three early examples at Chichester are incised, and one of them is surrounded by the indents for a brass inscription in separate letters. A well-known indent in Dorchester, Oxfordshire, shows an arm appearing from the side of the slab and grasping the crozier, and at Ainderby, Yorkshire, the crozier is leaning against a cross. There are other examples at Horspath, Oxfordshire, an early one to an abbot (Fig 2); Thornton Abbey, Yorkshire, where there is a curious device resembling a keyhole above the crozier; and Lesnes Abbey, Kent, where the slab is inscribed ABBAS ELYAS and the number IX, indicating the ninth abbot.[15] There seems to have been a very elaborate one encircled by coronets in St Paul's, and at Peterborough an early brass showing a crozier and a mitred head on either side of a cross.

Abbesses do not seem ever to have been as common as abbots, but there were two simple ones at Romsey Abbey, Hampshire; an elaborate canopied brass at Wingfield, Suffolk, to the Lady Catherine, Abbess of Barking; and two at Laycock. One of these commemorated Ela, Countess of Salisbury, foundress and Abbess of Laycock, who died in 1261, though the indent looks as if it was made c1320.

There were many brasses to other church dignitaries in cathedrals, particularly York and Lincoln: we find references to brasses of succentors, procurators, vicars choral, deans, archdeacons, canons, chaplains, chancellors, subdeacons, treasurers, chantry priests, prebendaries, cantors, sub-treasurers, precentors and vice-chancellors, as well as sacristans and vergers. The majority of these would have been shown in priestly vestments, though sacristans and vergers would have been in minor orders and probably only wearing a cassock. Deacons and subdeacons should have been shown in the vestments proper to their rank, the dalmatic and tunicle respectively, but there is no certainty that there were ever figure brasses to these orders. There is a fragment of a deacon's brass on the back of a palimpsest at Burwell, Cambridgeshire, but this is probably foreign.

Peculiar dignities were conferred at St Paul's and Windsor. At the former some canons had the style of canons cardinal, and there were mid-fifteenth-century brasses to four of them side by side at the entrance to St Faith's church in the crypt.[16] At Windsor the canons formed the chapter of the Order of the Garter, and wore the mantle of the Order. Three or four survive in other churches, but no less than eleven are recorded by Ashmole as having formerly existed in St George's Chapel. Other forms of ecclesiastical brass show priests vested in the cassock alone, as at Chalfont St Peter, Buckinghamshire, and Broxbourne, Hertfordshire, both recently lost; and vested for a funeral, as at Upwell, Norfolk, a fellow to the one surviving there.

Brasses to members of the religious orders naturally suffered much during the dissolution of the monasteries, though in fact there do not seem ever to have been very many. Brasses of Benedictines have been lost from St Alban's; Christchurch, Hampshire; and Boxgrove, Sussex. A monk in Benedictine habit recently discovered on the back of a palimpsest at Isfield, Sussex, was probably a Cluniac from Lewes, since we know that spoil from Lewes was taken to Isfield. Dorchester Abbey has indents for two Augustinian canons. Despite the fact that Carthusians are not supposed to have personal monuments, there was one at Sheen, Middlesex, to Dom John Ingylby, 1499, Prior of Sheen and Bishop of Llandaff. It survives as a palimpsest at Edlesborough, Buckinghamshire.

St James's, Clerkenwell, had a brass to the last Prior of the Order of St John, William Weston, 1540. A drawing by Schnebbelie made before the church was rebuilt in 1788 showed the altar tomb with a carved recumbent cadaver, and indents for a kneeling brass figure and achievement.[17] Fragments of a very fine figure of a prior of the same order have been pieced together by Mr Page-Phillips from palimpsests in several different churches.[18]

Until recently the only surviving full-length brass to a friar was the one at Great Amwell, Hertfordshire, but this was stolen in 1968 and rather inadequately restored. Other brasses to Franciscans are known from Durham (now Trinity) College, Oxford, and possibly Middleham, Yorkshire. A curious palimpsest at St John Sepulchre, Norwich, shows an anchorite behind a grille, apparently in a Carmelite habit.

Of nuns other than abbesses the only lost examples seem to be a demi-figure at Romsey, and the curiously late example at Clerkenwell, which survived until 1788. The latter showed Isabel Sackvile, the last Prioress, in her habit, but was engraved at her death in 1570.[19]

Turning to the laity, we find that royalty and the higher nobility are totally unrepresented on surviving brasses, save for the insignificant brass of Katherine of Aragon, and the well-known half-effigy of King Ethelred. There are or were several indents which were pointed out as belonging to British or Saxon royalty, and remembering the Ethelred brass, it is not impossible that such brasses could have been made in the Middle Ages. King Didanus and Queen Safrida, the parents of St Frideswide, were supposed to be the figures on the great chantry chapel and watching loft in Oxford Cathedral, though the indents suggest a judge and wife of c1460. Gough mentions indents for King Anna and his son Firminus at Blythborough, Suffolk, but suggests they really commemorate two late fifteenth-century knights. The brasses of King Arthur and Queen Guenevere at Glastonbury have already been discussed. As for King Lucius at Winchester, Gough pertinently remarks that his tomb 'ought to be left undetermined till the reality of the king himself be settled'.[20] We are on firmer ground with King Ina of Wessex (688-725) at Wells, since a surviving sketch of 1794 by John Carter shows a brass of the early fourteenth century which could well have been laid in his memory.[21]

There were certainly contemporary brasses to princes of the blood royal. The indents survive on two small altar tombs in the Confessor Chapel of Westminster Abbey for Princess Margaret, 1472, and Princess Elizabeth, 1495; Dingley mentions a brass to Prince Edward, 1471, at Tewkesbury, and Browne Willis one to Prince Arthur, 1502, at Worcester. Beaulieu, Hampshire, has the remains of a fine inlaid incised slab to Princess Eleanor, 1311.

Among royal dukes was the magnificent and remarkable brass to Thomas of Woodstock, Duke of Gloucester and son of Edward III, 1397, in Westminster.[22] At Fotheringay, Northamptonshire, there was one to Edward, Duke of York, killed at Agincourt in 1415, of which a scrap of brass survives. Other ducal brasses in evidence were an inscription to Charles, Duke of Suffolk, 1545, at St George's, Windsor; one to Thomas Howard, second Duke of Norfolk, 1524, at Thetford, Norfolk (moved to Lambeth at the Dissolution); and a remarkable brass to Humphrey, Duke of Buckingham, 1460, and his Duchess, at Pleshey, Essex. Among duchesses represented were two wives of John of Gaunt at Lincoln and a third at Newark, a Duchess of Norfolk at Lambeth, and a fine surviving indent for Isabel of Castile, wife of Edmund, Duke of York, 1393, at King's Langley, Hertfordshire.

Earls seem always to have been poorly represented, but there were two magnificent early brasses to countesses in monasteries—Ela of Warwick at Osney, whose brass of 1297 is described by Leland, and Ela of Salisbury at Laycock, already mentioned. Knights on the whole are very well represented on surviving brasses, but there have been disproportionate losses from the early period. Cross-legged or mail-clad knights have been lost from the following: St Mary's, Chester, with ailettes; Shalford, Essex; Canterbury Cathedral (Sir William Septvans, 1323); Emneth, Norfolk, with canopy and Coronation of the Virgin; Linwood, Lincolnshire (Sir Henry de Bayous, c1335, Fig 17); Norton Disney in the same county (Sir William d'Iseni, 1335); Peterborough Cathedral (Sir Gascelin de Marham, of which a drawing survives in the British Museum); Hawton, Nottinghamshire (Sir Robert de Compton, 1308); Leatheringham and Stoke by Nayland, Suffolk, the latter dated 1318 and canopied; Aston Rowant, Oxfordshire (Sir Hugh le Blount, 1326); and Burton Agnes, Yorkshire (a curious brass to Sir Roger Somerville, 1336). Other slightly later knights holding shields were once to be seen at Hallingbury, Essex; Whaddon, Cambridgeshire; Brabourne, Kent; and Barrowby, Lincolnshire. An indent formerly at Drayton Basset, Staffordshire, showed a knight of c1350 brandishing a spear with a pennon.

Brasses to Knights of the Garter included Sir William Kingston, 1540, in full robes at Painswick, Gloucestershire, and an early one at St Paul's Cathedral. Shields encircled by the Garter appear on indents to knights at Salisbury and Rochester Cathedrals and at East Balsham, Norfolk, and to a bishop at Winchester. Chingford, Essex, and St Neot's, Huntingdonshire, had brasses to Yeomen of the Guard in their liveries, holding pole-axes. A very odd form of livery collar shown on a brass at Mildenhall, Suffolk, comprised a chain holding a small coronet encircling a hound.

An important profession now totally unrepresented on brasses was that of Officers of Arms. Most of them seem to have been in London, which may explain the unusually heavy losses. St Paul's contained the brass of Sir Payne Roet, Guyenne King at Arms, of the late fourteenth century, which is mentioned by Weever as already mutilated. A Norroy King at Arms, Lawrence Dalton, 1561, lay in St Dunstan in the West and Clarenceux Kings at St Helen's, Bishopsgate, 1529, and St Olave's, Hart Street, 1428. At Middle Claydon,

Buckinghamshire, on the back of a later brass is an inscription to Walter Bellingham, Ireland King of Arms, 1487, probably plundered from a London church. There was a York Herald at St Dunstan in the West, and another on an incised slab at Reculver, Kent. Drawings survive of nearly all of these, showing the figures in civil dress with the tabard, and the Kings crowned and with sceptres. The finest seem to have been the one in St Olave's, with his feet on a lion, and one of those at St Dunstan's, with a pendant portcullis on his breast and two more crowns flanking his head.[23]

Many other professions were formerly represented on brasses. Oxford had three brasses to beadles of the various faculties holding their staves, in the University Church and All Saints'; there was a gamekeeper, Gilbert Gilpyn, 1500, in hunting costume with horn and hound at Woking, Surrey; and Weever asserts that there was a brass in Hackney Church to a milkmaid, Alice Ryder, 1517, 'her portraiture in brasse with a milk pale upon her head', though this seems rather unlikely. Other professions mentioned on brasses formerly in cathedrals were often those of retainers of the church—organists at Durham, St Alban's and York; a bellringer at St Paul's; a cook at Lincoln; and a goldsmith , a master carpenter, and, most interestingly for us, a lattoner or brass engraver, William Bradley, 1505, at York. His inscription reads, *'armigeri et latonii quondam magistri cementariorum hujus ecclesie metropolit. Ebor.'*, and evidently he was a man of some importance, doubtless the owner of the York workshop that produced many local brasses at this date.

UNUSUAL BRASSES

A surprisingly high proportion of lost brasses seem to have been odd or unusual in different ways. Many of the peculiarities found on indents are in the canopies. The standard canopy is an ogival arch supported on pinnacled shafts; the

168

shafts may be doubled, the space filled with niches, and the main arch doubled or trebled, or surmounted by a flat-topped super-canopy. Variations and deviations from this are eccentric, as in the unusual use of the standard form at Hurley, Berkshire, where a double canopy covered two half-effigies, when normally those who could afford canopies would have had full-length figures (Plate 4a). There was another at Merton College, Oxford, where a single canopy of normal form spanned two figures.

Some more unusual forms of construction are found in the following examples. At Horsheath, Cambridgeshire, the lost canopy of a surviving effigy had double shafts linked at the top by round-headed arches, on each of which was an angel; from the angels' backs rose a straight-sided chevron-like canopy, with pinnacles at the angles and half-way up the sloping sides. At Hawkesbury Upton, Gloucestershire, a very fine indent to Thomas de Upton, Abbot of Pershore, 1413, has a triple canopy, the central pediment supporting a Virgin and Child, above which is a second ogival canopy, supported on the intermediate pinnacles and linked to the tops of the side-shafts by flying buttresses; on either side of this super-canopy were branches supporting figures of saints. The whole composition is about 4m long. At Nether Wallop, Hampshire, another indent of an abbot has a regular canopy with super-canopy, and four straight projections leading off to the edge of the slab. It has been suggested that we have here half of a double slab, with two canopies linked by 'bridges'.

The canopy at Connington, Huntingdonshire, has already been mentioned in connection with the crucifix forming the central shaft. Its two pediments are straight-sided, not ogival, there is no central pinnacle, and the side shafts form part of the marginal inscription, which turns and runs across the top of the slab. This last peculiarity is also shown on a fragment of a slab now built into a doorway in the tower of the former St Martin's, Oxford. At Gillingham, Kent, a double canopy with super-canopy over a knight and wife is flanked by two miniature canopies, doubtless for their children. One of the oddest of all was at Westminster Abbey, where the brass of Thomas of Woodstock was divided up into seventeen almost equal-sized compartments by very elaborate canopy work, filled with figures of the Trinity, saints, the Duke and Duchess, the King and Queen and all their children and relations. There were other odd canopies at Loughborough, Leicestershire; the Austin Friary, London; King's Lynn and Ingham, Norfolk; Exton, Rutland; and St Alkmund's, Shrewsbury.

A curious indent at East Balsham, Norfolk, unfortunately badly worn, shows a large armed figure of the late fourteenth-century leaning heavily over to his left, overshadowing a diminutive armed figure, probably his son. Odd spaces are filled in with gartered shields and a helmet, and a normal triple canopy covers them.

Combined brasses of two knights are not common. Other unusual combinations of figures were two priests together at Great Marlow, Buckinghamshire; a knight and a priest together at Pleshey, Essex (Fig 23), and at Belchamp Walter in the same county; a knight, a civilian and one wife between them at Cookham, Berkshire; and, according to Torre, a priest and a woman at York—'In the midst are kneeling at prayer a Canon shaven on his crown & a Woman respecting him, & 2 children on each side of them.'[24]

Depictions of the deceased both alive and as a skeleton or corpse are much rarer on brass than in stone, but lost examples include one at York to John Gisburgh, precentor, 1481, 'a large Effigies of a Clergyman . . . Below that is another little Image of the Defunct lying in a Winding Sheet cross the stone'.[25]

A large number of brasses showed animals of different kinds. The late Major Evans published a collection of elephants on brasses, to which can be added one supporting a cross at Tilty, Essex.[26] Most animals appear at the feet of effigies, and unusual ones formerly existed at Maidstone (an eagle at the feet of a woman); Pluckley, Kent (a colt at the man's feet and a lion at his wife's); and St Margaret's, King's Lynn (a rabbit or coney at the feet of Walter Coney). The choice of the eagle and colt was heraldic, as was that of the other peculiar beasts found on surviving brasses-unicorns, porcupines or gryphons. At Whaddon, Cambridgeshire, a remarkable indent, c1360, shows the dog and lion at the feet of the figures separated from them by a gap large enough for shields to be inserted, which rather defeats the object of having animals beneath effigies to round off the composition and provide a solid block for the feet.

The significance of birds on lost brasses is rather more puzzling. A large indent at Canterbury to Archbishop Henry Dean, 1503, has four small birds looking rather like ducklings on either side of the main figure. Upwell, Norfolk, has indents for two large long-beaked birds, with inscriptions but no other accessories, and these seem to parallel the surviving bird at Old Buckenham, though it is still not clear what sort of bird they were and why they should appear on brasses. At Redbourne, Hertfordshire, two brasses to the Pecok family were each distinguished by a peacock as a rebus, but only fragments of one of the birds survive. The lost brass in St Paul's to Richard Lichfild, 1496, shows two large birds holding scrolls (Fig 6).

Three early indents show peculiar devices that many have tried to see as some sort of animal. They appear scattered at random, and inverted or on their sides, accompanied by little stars, over the surface of surviving indents at Saltwood, Kent, 1311, and Trotton, Sussex, c1318 (the figure surviving), and on the lost brass of Ralph de Hengham, 1308, from St Paul's (Fig 5). In the last instance Hollar drew them as sheep, but it seems likely that they were already lost by his time, and he was simply trying to make sense of the peculiar indents remaining. One of these devices is reproduced in the hope that some suggestion as to its significance may be made (Fig 28).

A similar scatter of stars, but with crescents instead of the other devices, is shown on a slab to Bishop William Rede, 1385, at Chichester. He is supposed to have been an astrologer, but it is not clear whether this is simply a conjecture based on the indent.

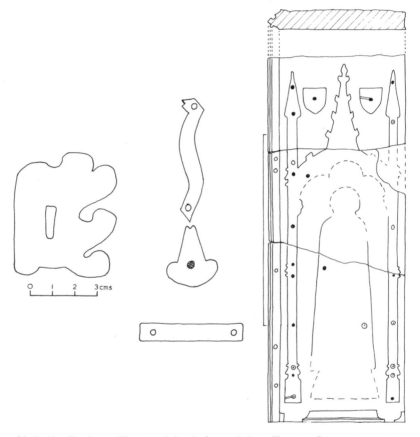

28 (*left*)   Device, still unexplained, from slab at Trotton Sussex, comparable to those at Saltwood, Kent, and St Paul's Cathedral
29 (*centre*)   Praying hands with scroll, c1450, St Mary the Virgin, Oxford
30 (*right*)   Possibly a priest in cope under canopy, c1440, now in churchyard at West Grinstead, Sussex. The slab has formed the top of an altar tomb, and is moulded on two edges

Emblems of various kinds are shown on a number of indents. The chalice as a symbol for a priest is well represented on surviving brasses, and it is used as a contrast to the shield on the double brass at Pleshey to the knight and priest divided by a pillar (Fig 23). An indent at New College, Oxford, shows a doctoral cap or *pileus* suspended over the head of the effigy by angels. A professional symbol was a bell, used for bell-founders at Barking, Essex, and St Martin's, Leicester. Other emblems were placed as rebus devices punning on the name, like the peacocks for Pecok and the salmon for the Saloman family at South Weald, Essex. At Salisbury two fine slabs to the Hungerford family were powdered with sickles, the family badge. A skull was shown on an indent at New College, and a figure of Death appeared on a lost brass at Lowestoft illustrated by Cotman.

The rose was a common device, usually as a symbol of the Virgin Mary, though it could be used for profane love as opposed to the lily for sacred love. It is not clear whether it was used as a political badge on brasses, though very small roses dimidiated with suns in splendour appear on the brasses of some Yorkist supporters. Large inscribed roses formerly existed at Bolnhurst, Bedfordshire; Weeke, Hampshire; St Alban's Abbey; and St Peter's, St Albans. The last is preserved in direct impressions bound into the Introduction to Volume II of Gough's *Sepulchral Monuments,* as well as in several successful attempts at reversing the prints so that the writing is legible, in the manuscript material in the Bodleian.[27] It is inscribed across the stamens *'Ecce',* and around them in a circle *'qd' expedi habui qd' donavi habeo qd' negavi puni^{or} qd Svavi p'didi* and the English translation, 'Lo al y^t eu' J spēt y^t sū t^{i}me had J Al y^t J Zaf i g^{o}d etet y^t n^{o}w have J y^t J ney' zaf ne lēt y^t now abie J y^t J kepetil J wet y^t lost Y' (Lo, all that ever I spent, that some time had I, All that I gave in good intent, that now have I, That I neither gave nor lent, that now aby I [ie I am punished] That I kept till I went, that lost I).

The brass of Abbot Kirton, 1466, at Westminster had a large rose on the canopy, explicity in honour of the Virgin and inscribed MARIA on the petals. Gough illustrates it and tells us that the effigy had 'at his feet two eagles holding a scroll inscribed *Eleyson kyrie curando morbida mundi'*.[28] Two large pontifical brasses, an unknown bishop or prior at Winchester, c1430, and Archbishop Dean at Canterbury, 1503, had large roses at the corners of the marginal inscription, probably enclosing evangelistic symbols like those surviving at Ely.

Scrolls, twisted or otherwise arranged, formed the principal features of a number of brasses that have mostly been lost because of their fragility. Some compositions were made up entirely of such scrolls, as at Minster Lovel, Oxfordshire, where fragments survive, though the slab and original arrangement are lost. A similar composition commemorated Archbishop Scot at York, and a late brass on much the same lines seems to have existed at Swerford, Oxfordshire. Scrolls were much more commonly scattered all over the surface of the slab, between figures, canopies and the like. There is a good surviving example at Wiston, Sussex, but they were lost from Endellion, Cornwall; Gestingthorpe, Essex; St Peter's, St Albans; Launde, Leicestershire; Lincoln Cathedral (Fig 27); King's Lynn; and St Mary's, Lambeth.

Scrolls were also used in more idiosyncratic ways to surround an effigy. St Stephen's, Norwich, had a shroud brass to a priest surrounded by a circular arrangement of four scrolls.[29] At Potton, Bedfordshire, there was a chalice surmounted by a small scroll and enclosed by a long one folded to make a lozenge-shaped frame, the whole set in a carved stone frame on the wall. Another chalice, at Fakenham, Norfolk, was enclosed by two scrolls twisted into a heart shape, with the inscription round them.[30] An indent formerly at Little Wittenham, Berkshire, showed a woman whose head was surrounded by a circular scroll, twisted into pleats at the top and sides to give an impression rather like a cross head.[31]

A form of scroll brass, for which no parallels survive, took the form of a prayer scroll rising from a hand or pair of hands. There is a very fine indent for one in St Mary's, Oxford (Fig 29), and there was another at Hadleigh, Suffolk, with only a single hand, which was described in the mid-nineteenth-century as 'representing a man's hand and a serpent near the middle finger of it. Tradition asserts that it commemorated one Henry Mole, of Pond Hall, who was bitten in that part by an adder and died of the wound.' In a footnote Haines corrected this, and instanced a parallel at Elmden, Essex, where the hands emerged from clouds. The original author, however, stuck to the adder version, maintaining that the tradition was of very long standing in the neighbourhood.[32] A rubbing in the Gough collection shows two open hands in association with an inscription to John Dawson, 1531, at Northwold, Norfolk, which may similarly have been furnished with scrolls.[33]

Among heraldic peculiarities now lost were a few brasses showing banners instead of shields. One at Fyfield, Essex, consisted of a plain cross, the arms terminated by fleurs de lys, with a banner on each side, and elsewhere they appear as part of large compositions, as at Tewkesbury, and on some surviving brasses. A much odder brass was the shield at Stanton Harcourt, Oxfordshire, supposed to date from 1293 but lost since 1860, which showed a dimidiated coat of arms, unique on brass and rare in heraldry. Apparently the field of the arms was cut away so that the stone showed between the charges. Luckily several rubbings survive, and it was illustrated in Haines's *Manual* (p 121).

A fine cross brass at Tormarton, Gloucestershire, also illustrated by Haines (p 124), commemorated the founder of the church, and showed a large model of the church behind his head. The figure stands in the head of the cross, which appears to be precariously balanced on a tabernacle-a good example of the uncertainty among the designers of brasses whether the compositions were to be seen as vertical or horizontal.

Losses have been unduly heavy among Flemish brasses imported into England and still more so in Scotland. The slabs of Tournai marble have already been mentioned, and those that show indents for separately inlaid brasses include types of which there is no surviving example even abroad. There are several ecclesiastics, as at Chichester, Malden in Essex, Boston in Lincolnshire and Aberdeen Cathedral; knights, as at Iona Cathedral; a lady at Sefton Chapel, East Lothian; and a nun at North Berwick. The majority were not simple brasses but incised slabs with various parts inlaid or accentuated in brass. Usually the hands and feet were inlaid, but existing slabs show indents for saints in canopies, in addition to chalices, shields, inscriptions and evangelistic symbols. One slab at Boston shows an incised priest in Mass vestments, with the orphreys and apparels of the vestments inlaid. On the other hand there were brasses, such as a knight at Dundrennon Abbey, which had the faces inlaid in stone. Eighteen Flemish quadrangular plates have been lost from Scotland, and at least five large ones from England.

Small Flemish brasses of the type now represented by the Aveley brass are less common. One survives at Boston, but it is completely effaced and might as well be lost; and two more were lost, from St Alkmund's, Shrewsbury, and Little Shelford, Cambridgeshire. The latter is known from a rubbing in the Cambridge Museum, which shows the figure of Elena de Freville, 1380, against a plainly diapered background under a simple square-topped canopy.[34] The one at Shrewsbury showed a civilian and wife, Simon and Joan Walsche, under a double canopy.[35] All had inscriptions across the bottom on plates very much wider than the figure brasses. There is a very similar one, c1350, on the back of an inscription of 1403 at Great Bowden, Leicestershire; the early re-use implies that the original brass was in England, not Continental spoil.

Many indents are now to be found out of doors, where they have been placed by unsympathetic architects (Fig 30), but some were intended to be external, usually mounted on the outside walls of churches. An early sixteenth-century indent for a family group may be seen on the outside of the south wall of the nave at Tewkesbury. At St Peter's, Dorchester, Dorset, a brass was set on the wall of a cottage overlooking the churchyard. Brasses were fixed to churchyard tombs at Houghton Conquest, Bedfordshire; and in the Subdeanery cemetery, Chichester. The porches at Blewbury and Sonning, Berkshire, and Worcester Cathedral, had indents for mural family groups.

Many peculiar or unusual forms of brasses can be detected from indents, but for unusual inscriptions we usually have to rely on documentary sources. Very few of the separate-letter inscriptions that can be read from indents are of any intrinsic interest, as most give only the name and ask for prayers. Among later inscriptions some are peculiar for their wording or information, as, for instance, at Shinfield, Berkshire, to John Felowe, c1450: '*Quondam Theodore honorat' de Wallyngford'.*[36] This means, 'Once an inhabitant of the Honour of Wallingford', and employs a unique Latinised form of the Middle English *Theodise,* an inhabitant. Braceborough, Lincolnshire, has probably the only reference on a brass to the Black Death: Thomas and Joan le Wasteneys *'le quel morust en le graund pestilence l'an de grace 1349'.*[37]

At Pusey, Berkshire, the inscription to Richard Pusey states that he, 'Having in his Lyfe Time received whole Christ, that is, not only as a Prophet and Priest, but as Lord and King too, in this true justifying Fatih, dyed most comfortably, Aug the iid. A.D. MDLIII', (error for 1653, from Ashmole).

At Ilford, Essex, there is the following:

Here lieth the body of Sir John Smyth sumtyme maister of this place a good house holder a Fyne Manne large in almys he did Worshippe to all hys kynne-all the felosshippe was the Meryer that Sir John Smyth was inne: I pray to god have Mercy on hys soule & all Christen. he passed to god the xi⁰ day of November in the yere of Grace A M⁰ CCCC LXXV For charite say a pater noster ave.[38]

At Enfield, Middlesex, the inscription to Anne Gery, 1643,
is in verse:

> Here lies enterr'd
> One that scarce err'd
> A virgin modest, free from foly,
> A virgin knowing, patient, holy,
> A virgin blest with beauty here
> A virgin crown'd with glory there.
> Holy virgins, read and say
> We shall hither all one day.
> Live well, yee must
> Be turn'd to dust.[39]

REDATING AND NAMING BRASSES

Research into lost brasses has not only told us much about the
study of brasses in general and about types and forms now
lost, but it has also in several cases led to the discovery of
more evidence about surviving brasses, particularly in the
matter of supplying names and dates. For example, in
researching for the survey of lost brasses in Oxford we were
able to produce a date for the brass of George Lassy at Magdalen, formerly given as c1500 but in fact 1496. Similarly the
brass in St Peter le Bailey, which is undated and gives the
names simply as G. and M. Box, was found to commemorate
George and Margaret Box, 1665. More importantly, an
anonymous academic figure at Magdalen, usually attributed
to Thomas Dyke, 1503, was shown on a rubbing in the Hinton
collection to be Richard Barns of 1499, a much more appro-
priate date for it to join its fellows in the small local workshop
that operated at this time in Oxford. The indent in Merton
College, already mentioned, is so similar to an undated surviving brass that it can be confirmed that what has in fact
always been its approximate date is accurate.

The Septvans brass at Chartham was first redated after
Ralph Griffin and Mr Greenhill discovered the 'ghost' of the

other Septvans brass in Canterbury. The latter was presumed to commemorate Sir William de Septvans, 1323, and it was deduced that both had been made at the same time.[41]

As research into lost brasses continues, it is to be hoped that many more of these as it were accidental benefits will accrue. Far too many named brasses are still undated, not to mention loose figures and stray pieces of brass now in museums that have never been traced to their original churches. A good example of the sort of research that can be carried out was provided by Dr Cameron when examining a lot of loose brasses in a saleroom in 1961.[42] An armoured figure that had been drifting about England attached to an oak table for about 100 years was identified as one from Peckleton, Leicestershire, illustrated by Nichols. Similarly an angel was identified as the missing one from Elsing, despite the fact that the loose one had no halo and the angel surviving at Elsing had. Reference to Ord's impression and Cotman's engraving proved that the irregularity was genuine, and the angel did indeed belong to Elsing. In this case the loose brass has been generously returned to its slab.

Many loose and unidentified brasses could very probably be identified and returned to their churches if a complete list of lost brasses could be compiled and indexed. Not all of them are to be found in museums or private possession, several have found their way into churches to which they do not belong, such as a coped priest of c1480 from Barnes that has been for the last 60 years in St Peter's, Clapham.

Notes to this chapter appear on page 188

7

THE FUTURE

And nothing will be shortly left to continue the memory of the
deseased to posteritie . . . (Weever)

As we saw at the end of Chapter 2, damage and loss of brasses
has by no means ceased. Since that chapter was written, a
figure has been stolen from Putney, two from Great Book-
ham, and an inscription from West Horsley, all in Surrey.
The demand for works of art for private collections or unscrupulous museums is increasing, and as more churches are
made redundant, their fittings lie open to theft or dispersal.
An alarming precedent has been created by which it seems
possible for churchwardens once again to sell their brasses,
this time not for their scrap value but in the art salerooms.
Gough quotes a court ruling of 1469 on the subject, when
Lady Wiche brought a suit against the parson of a London
church for removing the funeral achievements of her late
husband. Sir William Yelverton (whose brass is at Rougham,
Norfolk), ruled in her favour, that 'these are not intended as
either offerings or oblations, but were hung up in honour of
the party deceased, and therefore do not belong to the parson.
For (says he) I use to sit in the chancel, and I have brought
thither a carpet, a cushion, and a book; shall the parson have
these because they are brought into the chancel? I say no; no
more in the other case.'[1] Unfortunately in a parallel case
recently this judgement was overruled, and there seems to be

180

no legal impediment to the sale of funeral achievements and monuments, even from churches still in use.

Now that many churches are disused and liable to be declared redundant, brasses are even more likely to be sold out of them. If they are salvaged, it is usually at the expense of their slabs. To remove a brass from its slab is comparable not to unframing a picture but to cutting away the background of a portrait leaving the figure in silhouette. As funerary monuments, brasses are of course incomplete without the body they were designed to cover and the hallowed surroundings in which they were designed to lie. Where they must be removed from these, it does not seem too much to ask that at least they be kept as artistic unities and preserved with their slabs. In practice they are usually torn up and sent loose to the new parish church, or to a museum, where they can never have the same meaning or be as well appreciated as in their natural setting. In some redundant churches, however, they are simply abandoned, and presumably, when the building is demolished, will be carted away with the rubble. In at least one instance the brasses have found their way to a hotel near the site of a closed church and are nailed up on the staircase.

Even in surviving churches brasses are under threat, as alterations and improvements to the fabric, as well as the ever-increasing flow of visitors, cause new upheavals. To protect brasses from the feet of visitors, it is now normal to cover them with carpets, though this too has its disadvantages. An increasing number of churches have fitted carpets, and the brasses can only be seen by rolling up 50m of deep pile, which in many cases is forbidden or made impossible. One wonders what is the point of having brasses at all if they are covered in this way; they neither fulfil their original purpose as monuments nor can be appreciated as works of art. When they are uncovered, however, they are liable to be worn by passing feet or, much worse, polished by well-meaning church ladies. The simple solution would seem to be to cover brasses with small carpets, or with separate sections if the

181

church is carpeted throughout, so that they can be protected but still accessible.

Walking on brasses does not only wear them but also causes damage by pressure, which is of course not saved by carpeting at all. Pressure from feet or furniture will eventually loosen brasses by straining the junction of plate and rivet. Moreover, if the pitch backing to the brass is dried up and there is a hollow behind the plates (as with the majority of brasses), the pressure will cause the metal to flex up and down, which will weaken the structure of the metal and may cause the brass to crack up. This is incidentally the only sort of damage that brass-rubbing can cause, so that there can be no justification for forbidding brass-rubbing while allowing people to walk over floor brasses, however well carpeted.

The vexed question of whether brass-rubbing wears brasses has been finally settled by scientific experiment. It has been calculated that if a brass were rubbed three times a day for a century, it would be worn by 0.054mm; in other words, to wear out an engraved line 1mm deep would take 2,000 years.[2] No brass, of course, is ever rubbed that much, and there is no threat from wear to any brass from brass-rubbing. Indeed, if a brass is being rubbed, it is at least being protected from being walked on. The vicar of Cobham wrote to *The Times* on 1 April 1972 to say that he welcomed brass-rubbers because they ensured that the church was watched, and the brasses were much less liable to be damaged by careful rubbing than by casual visitors wandering round an empty church. There have certainly been cases where brass-rubbers have saved churches from vandalism. However, it must be conceded that brass rubbing must be limited simply from the point of view of the use of the church, as well as because carelessness or accidents during rubbing may cause damage.

The present method of limiting brass-rubbing by charging a fee is not satisfactory. Fees are now so high that one can be certain that the only people who will pay them are those who are going to sell the rubbings-precisely the class of brass-rubber that is most likely to damage the brass or behave disrespectfully in the church. The serious chalcologist who wants a collection of brass-rubbings to study cannot possibly pay a fee of a pound or more for each rubbing. The arguments for charging a fee are usually that it 'deters all but serious rubbers', though it does precisely the opposite, or that 'the brasses are being exploited'. If the brasses are being exploited, it is no proper response for the churches to join in the exploitation, and it is nothing short of hypocritical and unworthy of a Christian church to charge the sort of fees that are now common.

Perhaps the problem resolves itself into what is the function of the Church of England. Is it a religious body or the caretaker of a national museum? Obviously the function of any church must be religious, and it is simply the bad luck of the Anglican church in England, as of the Catholic Church in Italy, to be burdened with a priceless national heritage. The revenues of the church should be spent on almsgiving, missions and the maintenance of the clergy, not on stones and brass. Clergy should be appointed for preaching and ministering, not as museum curators. It is unfair on the clergy to expect them to cope with the technicalities of archaeological conservation.

This having been said, it is clear that we should look elsewhere for both the funds and the expertise to maintain and repair brasses both in existing churches and in those no longer needed by their parishes. One could argue that, since all church revenues and the buildings themselves were seized by the state some 400 years ago, it is not unreasonable to expect the state to do its share in maintaining churches and their fittings.

State aid could prevent brasses ever being sold or dispersed from churches officially, though it is more difficult to guard against private theft. The most obvious precaution is to ensure that brasses are kept well secured to their slabs and not allowed to come loose, nor be fixed only with screws which anyone can undo. One of the recently stolen Surrey brasses was noticed to be completely loose beforehand, but the incumbent, though warned, took no steps to secure it. Locking churches is of no use whatsoever; neither professional art thief nor determined vandal would be kept out for more than a few minutes, and once in would be safe from interruption. A locked church is probably less secure than an unlocked one, and a great inconvenience to congregation and visitor alike.

Once brasses have been stolen it is rare that they can be recovered, even when they are openly offered for sale. This problem applies to all works of art and archaeological artefacts, and can only be solved by radical new legislation on antiquities, preferably on an international basis. Meanwhile all one can do is watch salerooms and art dealers and hope that stolen brasses are recognised before they can be sold. Rubbings or good illustrations of brasses would be essential to prove the identity of any disputed loose brass.

Despite all precautions, brasses will continue to disappear, and indents will be destroyed or covered with cement in the course of repairs or alterations. It is desirable to preserve all surviving brasses, though we must often abandon indents. There is no excuse, however, for any more indents to be lost without adequate recording, as it has been shown that this can be done cheaply, quickly and easily. Once the survey of indents is completed for the country, we need take less care about the preservation of what are after all unattractive slabs that are of no interest to the majority of people.

The study of lost brasses is only beginning. As more brasses are lost it is also becoming, alas, an expanding subject!

Notes to this chapter appear on page 189

CHAPTER NOTES

MBS Trans: Transactions of the Monumental Brass Society
Oxford Journal: Oxford Journal of Monumental Brasses
CUABC Trans: Transactions of the Cambridge University Association of Brass Collectors

CHAPTER 1, pages 7-10
1   *Oxford Journal*, 2, 369
2   *MBS Trans*, 10, 369
3   *MBS Trans*, 11, 209-52, 321-79
CHAPTER 2, pages 11-42
1   Petition in the Archbishop's Visitation at Sittingbourne (11 October 1511); Register Folio 57, vi. Quoted in *Proceedings of the Society of Antiquaries*, 2nd Ser, 8, 442-4
2   *MBS Trans*, 10, 2
3   *Ibid*, 11, 42
4   *Surrey Archaeological Collections*, 58, 1-20
5   *MBS Trans*, 8, 246, see also Stow's *Survey*
6   Will quoted in Gawthorpe. *Brasses*, 50
7   Langland. 'Crede of Piers the Ploughman', 1. 997-1000
8   Gough. *Sep Mons*, Intro to Vol 1, cxxiii
9   Ibid, cxx
10   *Essex Archaeological Society Transactions*, 10, 16
11   Bodleian Library, MSS Don e 111, f 8
12   *MBS Trans*, 10, 384; 11, 308
13   *Sussex Archaeological Collections*, 21, 181
14   Nichols. *Leics*, Vol I, 370-1
15   3 & 4 Edw VI, c 10
16   Macklin. *Br of Eng*, 306; Bouquet. *Church Brasses*, 262; *Oxford Journal*, 1, 137
17   Macklin. *Mon Br*, 23
18   Weaver, 50
19   Proclamation printed in full in Weever, 50, Druitt, 308
20   *Sussex Notes & Queries*, 4
21   Weever, 427
22   Published in the *Camden Society Miscellany*, XVI (1936)
23   Wood. *University of Oxford*, Vol II, 174
24   Wood. *City of Oxford*, III, 125
25   Connor. *Somerset Brasses*, 76
26   *MBS Trans*, 7, 71
27   Ibid, 8, 30

28 *Mercurius Rusticus,* 206, 220, 225, 230, 247
29 Wood. *University of Oxford,* IV, 232
30 Journals of the House of Commons, ii, 279
31 Suffolk portion ed by John Henry Newman as appendix to Edw Wells. *Rich Man's Duty* (Oxford, 1840); Cambs portion in *Transactions of the Cambridge & Huntingdon Archaeological Society,* 3, 77-91
32 *Querula Cantabrigiensis,* 17
33 F. J. Varley. *Cambridge during the Civil War,* 29-45
34 Quoted in Haines. *Manual,* 256
35 Haines, 256
36 See H. F. O. Evans. 'Malicious Damage to Brasses', *MBS Trans,* 10, 186
37 *Wood's Life and Times,* Oxford Hist Soc (1891-4), ed A. Clark
38 Druitt, 31
39 Surtees Society, Vol 35, 333-4
40 J. J. Moore. *A Gossiping Guide to Oxford,* undated
41 Cotman, I, intro, x
42 *Archaeological Journal,* 13, 182
43 *Essex Transactions,* 8, 366-8
44 *Norfolk Archaeology,* 6, 25; cf Gough. *Sep Mons,* I, intro, cxxi
45 Thorpe. *Registrum Roffense,* 777
46 *CUABC Trans,* 1, 19
47 Gough. *Sep Mons,* I, cxx; cf Britten. *Hist of Heref Cath,* 55
48 Fordyce. *History of Durham,* Vol I, 283
49 *Gent's Mag* (1805), 820
50 Nichols. *Leics,* III, pt i, pl 75, 515
51 Bodleian MSS DD Par Oxford All Saints a 1
52 See Gent's Mag Library, *English Topography,* VI, 176-81
53 Bodleian MS Top Berks c 49, f 171
54 Haines. *Manual,* II, 141
55 *Archaeological Journal,* 1, 208; cf Macklin. *Br of Eng,* 309
56 Gough. *Sep Mons,* I, intro, cxxi. Means Leatheringham
57 Nichols. *Leics,* IV, 356
58 *Essex Transactions,* NS, 8, 234
59 Bodleian Library MS Don e 109, f 28v
60 Creeny. *Continental Brasses,* iii
61 *Archaeologia Cantiana,* 32, 36-75
62 Dunkin. *Cornish Brasses,* 98
63 *Oxford Manual,* cxii
64 *Proceedings of the Society of Antiquaries,* 2nd Ser, 8, 384
65 *CUABC Trans,* 1, 48
66 From Sir George Airy's autobiography (1896); in *MBS Trans,* 8, 319
67 *Oxford Journal,* 1, 110
68 R. Günther. *Brasses of Magdalen College, Oxford,* 20
69 Haines. *Manual,* 259
70 *CUABC Trans,* 1, pt 7, 24
71 *Essex Trans,* 6, 4
72 *CUABC Trans,* 2, 69
73 Rev B. P. W. Stather Hunt. *Flinten History* (1953), 54
74 *MBS Trans,* 7, 65
75 Information supplied by Mr Carr of Kettering
CHAPTER 3, pages 43-75
1 *Oxford Journal,* 2, 154
2 *Archaeologia Cantiana,* 65, 137
3 *MBS Trans,* 11, 209, 321
4 *Home Counties Magazine,* 1, passim
5 Sadler. *West Sussex,* 12-40
6 *MBS Trans,* 11, 209, 321
7 For references see Mill Stephenson. *List*

8   *Home Counties Magazine,* 1, passim
9   Ralph Griffin. *Some Indents of Lost Brasses,* (private) (1914)
10 For photography of brasses see Norris & Kellett, Chap 4
11 See an account in Bouquet. *Church Brasses,* 234
12 Griffin. *Indents of Lost Brasses*
13 Bodleian Library MSS Gough Maps 226, f 28
14 *Oxford Journal,* 1, 113

CHAPTER 4, pages 76-115

1   PCC 30 Wattys, quoted in *MBS Trans* 5, 58
2   Winchester Probate Registry, quoted in *MBS Trans,* 6, 216
3   Quoted in *MBS Trans,* 4, 136, and Macklin, *B of Eng,* 9-10
4   See p 20, but given in full in *MBS Trans,* 9, 354
5   *Proceedings of the Society of Antiquaries of Scotland,* 6, 53
6   *Trans Cambridge & Huntingdon Archaeological Soc,* 3, 81
7   Gough, *Sep Mons,* ii, Intro, cccxxx
8   *Rites of Durham,* 107; quoted and the indent illust, Macklin. *Br of Eng,* 314
9   Court of Chivalry Law Report, *Antiquaries' Journal,* 19, 421-8
10 Ed by J. Harvey, Oxford Mediaeval Texts, 1969, 156 and 163
11 Leland, *Itinerary* (1909 ed): III, 264-5 (Bishop Wytto); I, 16 (Constance)
12 Gough. *Sep Mons,* I, Intro, xciv n; cf Connor. *Somerset,* 211
13 Leland. *Itinerary* (1909 ed): III, 226 (Bishop Lacey); III, 292 (Robert Burnell). Gough illustrates what he supposed to be Bishop Lacey's indent. *Sep Mons,* II, 367
14 Camden Society. *Miscellany,* XVI, NS, Vol 52 (1936), 6 and 63
15 Oxford Historical Society. *Collectanea,* IV (1909)
16 Camden Society, Vol 74 (1859): 124 ff (Blandford); 213 (Llandaff); 192 (Braunstone)
17 Bodleian Library, Gough Gen Top 55, facing p 11
18 Ibid, facing p 49
19 Greenhill, 40-1 and Plate IIIa; cf Gough. *Sep Mons,* II, lxxvii
20 Reproduced in *Surtees Society Records,* Vol 76, 222
21 William Cobbett. *Rural Rides* (9 April 1830); see *MBS trans.* 10, 494
22 Quoted Wagner. *Heralds & Heraldry in the Middle Ages,* 4
23 Printed as Appendix D to Wagner. *Heralds*
24 Bodleian Library, MS Wood D 14
25 Copy in Bodleian Library, MS Eng Misc, c 19; inscription, f 99
26 Gough. *Sep Mons,* II, Intro cccxx
27 Illustrated *MBS Trans,* 8, 260
28 *Kent Records, a Seventeenth Century Miscellany,* Kent Archaeological Society Publications, 17 (1960)
29 Ed of 1586 in Latin, Eng edn of 1695 (repr 1971, Newton Abbot); Gough's expanded ed, 1806
30 *A Survey of London* (1842 ed): 139 (Shirley); 94-5 (Knowles)
31 *MBS Trans,* 9, 160
32 Bodleian Library: 'Epitaphes out of the metropoliticall church and all the other parochial Churches wth in the most famous and Ancient Cytty of Yorke most Faithfully Collected by me Roger Dodsworthe the xij th of February A⁰ dñi 1618', MS Dodsworth 161; f17 (Langton); f21v (Ranulph)
33 *MBS Portfolio,* I, pt i, pl 3; W. Bentham. *Old St Paul's* (1902)
34 E. Ashmole. *Antiquities of Berkshire* (E. Curll, 1719)
35 See Bibliography. Notes by Hutton and Rawlinson are collated with Wood's in the City and County volumes
36 Bodleian Library, MS Aubrey 4, f 74
37 Ibid, 226-9. Inscription only of Bradbridge brass in Burrell
38 Original apparently lost; facsimile ed, Camden Society (1866-8)
39 *MBS Trans,* 11, 334-47
40 *Hearne's Collections,* Oxford Historical Society, 11 vols (1885-1918) III, 406 (St Cross inscription)

CHAPTER NOTES

41 See Bibliography
42 *Survey of York &c,* 377
43 Reproduced in Wright. *Brasses of Westminster Abbey,* 12; it was also engr in Sandford. *Genealogical History* (1677)
44 *MBS Trans,* 10, 93 (an earlier rubbing has since been found at Oxford)
45 Nichols, *Leics;* Launde, III, pl 46, fig 7, 328; Stanford, IV, pl 52, 356; Belgrave, III, pl 31, 178, fig c; Leatheringham, III, pl 75, 515
46 *MBS Trans,* 9, 80-91; 133-45
47 See Bibliography for full title and dates
48 *Gent's Mag,* (1792) pt II, 1091-2
49 Bodleian Library, MSS Rubbings Phillipps/Robinson 587-861, 876-933. See M. Clapinson. 'The Topographical Collections of Henry Hinton and James Hunt', *Oxoniensia,* 37, 215-20
50 See Bibliography. Two reproduced in Busby. *Companion Guide*
51 See Griffin. *Drawings,* and Griffin & Stephenson
52 Written in 1846, quoted *MBS Trans,* 5, 181
53 See Bibliography
54 *Sussex Archaeological Collections,* Vol 23 (1871), 129-92; 163 (Heathfield)
55 The rubbings catalogued are now in the Ashmolean Museum
56 See Winnington-Ingram. *Brasses in Hereford Cathedral,* 6

CHAPTER 5, pages 116-140
1 Oxford: *MBS Trans,* 11, 219-52; 321-79, Sussex: Sadler. *West and East Sussex,* and the author's observations. Surrey: Mill Stephenson's *Surrey.* Bedfordshire: H. K. St J. Sanderson. 'The Brasses of Bedfordshire', *MBS Trans.* Vol 2, 33, 74, 117, 153, 193, 275; Vol 3, 31. Huntingdonshire: H. W. Macklin. 'The Brasses of Huntingdonshire', *MBS Trans,* 3, 114, 167. Berkshire: Ashmole, and the Hinton MSS. Lincoln: *MBS Trans,* 2, 314; 3, 67, 119. St Paul's: Dugdale and *MBS Trans,* 2, 45. St Alban's: *Home Counties Magazine,* 1. York: Dodsworth, Drake and *MBS Trans,* 7, 342; 8, 1. Oxford and Chichester as City of Oxford and West Sussex
2 Page-Phillips. *Macklin's Monumental Brasses,* 126
3 *MBS Trans,* 10, 424; 11, 123
4 *MBS Trans,* 11, 2-12

CHAPTER 6, pages 141-179
1 Earlier German brasses, such as those at Augsberg (1187) and Verden (1231), are isolated examples and do not form part of any school, or the development of European brass work
2 The drawings are in the Bibliothèque Nationale and the Bodleian. Facsimile edition by M. Adhèmar
3 See Keblowski, plates 18-24. The brass at Lubiaz dated 1201 was engraved c1300 with the others; see op cit, 72-85
4 Royal Commission on Historical Monuments. *Westminster Abbey,* 26
5 *The Early Rolls of Merton College,* ed J. R. L. Highfield (Oxford Hist Soc, 1964), 137
6 RCHM. *Westminster Abbey,* 27
7 *MBS Bulletin,* No 5, 6-7
8 Ibid, No 3, 7-a provisional list of redated early brasses
9 The brass was probably engraved earlier, since the bishop 'being a zealous Papist, was turned out of his suffraganship' (Cotman, I, 33)
10 See the Passiontide hymn *Vexilla Regis* for the idea of Christ reigning from a tree *(regnavit a ligno Deus),* based on the Vetus Latinum version of Psalm 95, 10
11 This is not an historical event but a popular way of expressing the high honour in which Our Lady is held among the saints, a pre-eminence which to the medieval mind suggested queenship
12 Surtees Society, Vol 35, xvi-xviii
13 Horsfield. *History of Sussex,* I, 530; Sadler. *East Sussex,* 34-5
14 *MBS Trans,* 11, 308
15 Alfred W. Clapham. *Lesnes Abbey* (1915), 62, fig 9. Now in Erith

16 See very bad drawings of them by Dingley, ccccxxi
17 Bodleian Library, MS Gough Maps 225
18 Page-Phillips. *Macklin's Monumental Brasses,* 92
19 Illustrated in *Gent's Mag,* Vol 55, pt ii, 935
20 Gough. *Sep Mons,* I, Intro, lxxxix
21 Connor. *Somerset Brasses,* plate XXXVIII
22 Illustrated Wright. *Brasses of Westminster Abbey,* 12
23 That at St Olave's illustrated *MBS Trans,* 9, 301; that at St Dunstan's illustrated Surtees Society, Vol 122, frontis
24 *MBS Trans,* 7, 350
25 Ibid, 351
26 H. F. O. Evans. 'The Elephant on Brasses', *MBS Trans,* 10, 128
27 Bodleian Library, MS Gough Maps 223a
28 Gough. *Sep Mons,* II, pl lxxxi, 210
29 Cotman II, pl 107
30 Ibid, pl 105
31 Bodleian Library, MS Top Berks c 51, f 227
32 *Pro Suffolk Institute of Archaeology,* 3, 61, 288
33 Bodleian Library, MS Gough Maps 225
34 Illustrated in *MBS Trans,* 8, 221
35 Illust in *Trans Shropshire Archaeological Soc,* NS, 7, 411
36 Bodleian Library, MS Rubbings Phillipps/Robinson, 657
37 Quoted from Gough's MSS in Haines. *Manual,* 223
38 Illustrated *MBS Trans,* 3, 258
39 Quoted in *Trans of London & Middlesex Arch Soc,* 19, 167
40 *Archaeologia Cantiana,* 65, 137
41 *MBS Trans,* 10, 195-203
CHAPTER 7, pages 180-184
1 9 Edw IV, fol 15; quoted in Gough. *Sep Mons,* II, Intro cccxxv
2 *Nature* (15 June 1973), 243, 422

BIBLIOGRAPHY

Adhèmar, Jean. 'Les Tombeaux de la Collection Gaignières', *Gazette des Beaux Arts,* Tome I (Paris, 1974)

Ashmole, Elias. *Antiquities of Berkshire* (1719)

Beaumont, E. T. *Ancient Memorial Brasses* (Oxford, 1913)

Belcher, W. D. *Kentish Brasses,* 2 vols (1888, 1905)

Bertram, Jerome. *Brasses and Brass Rubbing in England* (Newton Abbot, 1971)

Bouquet, Dr A. C. *Church Brasses* (1956)

Boutell, Rev Charles, *Christian Monuments in England and Wales* (1854); *Monumental Brasses and Slabs* (1847); *The Monumental Brasses of England, a Series of Engravings on Wood* (1849)

Busby, Richard. *A Companion Guide to Brasses and Brass Rubbing* (1973)

Cambridge Camden Society. *Illustrations of Monumental Brasses* (1846)

Cambridge University Association of Brass Collectors. *Transactions* (1887-93). CUABC became the Monumental Brass Society

Camden, Sir William. *Britannia* (1586; Eng ed, 1695; repr Newton Abbot, 1971) See also enlarged ed by R. Gough (1806)

Cameron, Dr H. K. *A List of Monumental Brasses on the Continent of Europe* (1970); 'The Brasses of Middlesex', *Transactions of the London & Middlesex Archaeological Society* (1951, unfinished)

Christy, Miller, with Porteous, W. 'The Brasses of Essex' (originally in different journals; two parts published by the Monumental Brass Society (1948-51)

Clark, A. (ed). *Wood's Life & Times.* See Wood, Anthony

Connor, A. B. *Monumental Brasses in Somerset* (originally published in the *Somerset Arch Soc Proceedings,* 1931-53; reprinted in one vol, 1970)

Cotman, John. *Engravings of the most remarkable of the Sepulchral Brasses of Norfolk and Suffolk,* 2 vols (2nd ed, 1839)

Creeny, Rev W. F. *A Book of Facsimiles of Monumental Brasses on the Continent of Europe* (1884)

Dart, J. *History of Westminster Abbey,* 1742

Davidson-Houston, Mrs. 'Monumental Brasses in Sussex', *Sussex Archaeological Collections,* 76-80 (Lewes, 1936-40)

Davis, Cecil. *The Monumental Brasses of Gloucestershire* (Bath, 1899, repr 1969); 'The Monumental Brasses of Herefordshire and Worcestershire,' *Trans Birmingham & Midland Institute* (1844), 52

Dingley, Thomas. *An Historie from Marble* (c1685, Camden Society 1866-8)

Drake, Francis. *Eboracum or the History and Antiquities of York* (1736)

Dugdale, Sir William. *Antiquities of Warwickshire* (1656); *History of St Paul's* (1658)

Dunkin, E. H. W. *The Monumental Brasses of Cornwall* (1882)

Fisher, Thomas. *Collections Genealogical and Topographical for Bedfordshire* (1836); *Monumental Remains and Antiquities in Bedfordshire* (1828)

Franklyn, Julian. *Brasses* (1964)

Gawthorpe, W. J. *The Brasses of Our Homeland Churches* (1923)

Gentleman's Magazine, The (1731-1868)

Gittings, Clare. *Brasses and Brass Rubbing* (1970)

Gough, Richard. *Sepulchral Monuments in Great Britain, Applied to illustrate the History of Families, Manners, Habits and Arts, at the different periods from the Norman Conquest to the Seventeenth Century,* Part I and Introduction (1786); part II (1796); Intro to Part II (1802)

Greenhill, F. A. *The Incised Slabs of Leicestershire and Rutland* (Leicester, 1958)

——. *Incised Effigal Slabs* (1976)

Griffin, Ralph. *Some Indents of Lost Brasses* and *Drawings of Brasses in Some Kentish Churches* (privately printed, 1913-14); (with Mill Stephenson) *List of Monumental Brasses remaining in the county of Kent* (1922)

Günther, R. T. *Brasses in the Chapel of Magdalen College* (1914)

Gunton, Symon. *History of the Church of Peterborough* (1686)

Haines, Herbert. *Manual of Monumental Brasses* (1861, repr 1970)

Hammond, Lt. *Short Survey of the Western Counties* (1635, Camden Society 1936)

Hartshorne, Charles. *Sepulchral Monuments* (Cambridge, 1840)

Hearne, Thomas. *Collections* (Oxford Historical Society, 1885-1918)

Hollis, T. and C. *Monumental Effigies of Great Britain* (1840-42)

Hudson, F. *The Brasses of Northamptonshire* (1852)

Keblowski, Jan. *Pomniki Piastów Slaskich,* Ossolineum (1971)

Kent, J. P. C. 'Monumental Brasses, a New Classification of Military Effigies', *Journal of the British Archaeological Association,* 3rd Ser, 12, 70

Kite, Edward. *The Monumental Brasses of Wiltshire* (1860, repr Bath 1969)

Lewis, M. *Welsh Monumental Brasses* (Amgueddfa Genedlaethol Cymru, 1974)

Lysons, S. *Environs of London* (1796)

Macklin, Rev H. W. *The Brasses of England* (1907); *Monumental Brasses* (1890)

Manning, C. R. 'Lost Brasses', *Norfolk Archaeology,* 6, 3-24 (1861)

Mercurius Rusticus (1646), printed in *Angliae Ruina* (1648)

Monumental Brass Society Bulletin (1972 onwards)

Monumental Brass Society Portfolio (1894-1914, 1936 onwards)

Monumental Brass Society Transactions (1887-1914, 1936 onwards) See also CUABC

Morley, T. H. *Monumental Brasses of Berkshire* (1924)

Nichols, John. *Bibliotheca Topographica Britannica* (1780-95); *History of Leicestershire,* 4 vols (1795-1811)

Norris, Malcolm. *Brass Rubbing* (1964); *Monumental Brasses* (1976); (with Michael Kellett) *Your Book of Brasses* (1975)

Oxford Journal of Monumental Brasses (1897-1912)

Oxford Portfolio of Monumental Brasses (1898-1901, 1950-55)

Oxford Manual of Monumental Brasses (by Haines, Oxford, 1848)

Page-Phillips, John. *Children on Brasses* (1970); *Macklin's Monumental Brasses* (1969)

Querula Cantabrigiensis (1647), printed in *Angliae Ruina* (1648)

Registrum Fratrum Minorum Londinie. *Monumenta Franciscana,* I (Rolls Series); see also *Archaeological Journal,* 59, 258

Rites of Durham (1593; Surtees Society, II, Vol 107, 1903)

Sadler, A. C. *The Lost Monumental Brasses of East Sussex* (privately printed, 1970); *The Lost Monumental Brasses of West Sussex* (1969)

Sibun, Doris. *Dorset Brasses & the People they Commemorate* (Sherborne, 1974)

Simpson, Justin. *Sepulchral Brasses of England* (Stamford, 1857)

Spelman, Sir Henry. *The History and Fate of Sacrilege* (1632, 1698)

Stephenson, Mill. *A List of Monumental Brasses in the British Isles* (1926), *Appendix* (1938, repr 1964). 'The Monumental Brasses in Shropshire', *Trans of the Shropshire Arch Soc,* 2 Ser, 7, 381-450. *Monumental Brasses in Surrey,* originally in Surrey Arch Colls (1921, repr Bath, 1970). 'The Monumental Brasses of Yorkshire', *Yorkshire Archaeological Journal,* 12 (1893), 195-229; 15 (1898), 1-60, 119; 17 (1899), 1-81. See also with Ralph Griffin

Stothard, Charles. *Monumental Effigies* (1817)

Stow, John. *A Survey of London, contayning ye originall antiquity and increase, moderne estates, and description of that citie* (1598, 1842)

Suffling, E. R. *English Church Brasses* (1910, repr 1970)

Symonds, Richard. *Oxford Church Notes* (1643; Oxford Historical Society *Collectanea*, IV 1909); *Diary* (1643-4, Camden Society, Vol 74 1859)

Thorpe, John. *Custumale Roffense* (1788)

Victoria and Albert Museum. *Catalogue of Brass Rubbings* (1915; 2nd ed 1929)

Wagner, Sir Anthony. *Heralds and Heraldry in the Middle Ages* (Oxford, 1956)

Waller, J. G. and L. A. B. *A Series of Monumental Brasses from the Thirteenth to the Sixteenth Century* (1864, repr 1975)

Ward, J. S. M. *Brasses* (1912)

Way, Albert. 'Sepulchral Brasses and Incised Slabs', *Archaeological Journal*, 1 (1844), 187-212.

Weever, John. *Ancient Funerall Monuments* (1631)

Williams, Charles. 'Monumental Brasses in Warwickshire', *Trans of the Birmingham & Midland Institute* (1884), 16-51

Willis, Browne. *A Survey of the Cathedrals of York, Durham, Carlisle, Chester, Man, Litchfield, Hereford, Worcester, Gloucester & Bristol* (1727); *A Survey of the Cathedrals of Lincoln, Ely, Oxford & Peterborough* (1730); *History and Antiquities of the Town, Hundred & Deanery of Buckingham* (1755); and some monographs on Welsh cathedrals

Winnington-Ingram, A. J. *Monumental Brasses in Hereford Cathedral* (1956)

Wood, Anthony. *Athenae Oxoniensis* (1680); *Historia et Antiquitates Univ Oxon* (1674; Eng ed, by R. Gutch, 1791-6); *City of Oxford*, ed A. Clark (Oxford Hist Soc, 1881-99); *Parochial Collections* (Oxfordshire Record Soc, 1920-9); *Wood's Life & Times*, ed A. Clark (Oxford Historical Society, 1891-4)

Wright, J. S. N. *The Brasses of Westminster Abbey* (1969)

ACKNOWLEDGEMENTS

Thanks to John Blair for advice on the early brasses, especially those of the Lincolnshire school, to the Ashmolean Museum for the facilities to prepare Figs 4-6, 21, 23 and 24, and to various members of the Oxford University Archaeological Society for help and advice on the preparation of illustrations. Plate 2a and Figs 1, 3 and 29 are reproduced by permission of the University Vicar, Oxford.

INDEX